A Gentleman's Game
Reflections on Cricket History

Anindya Dutta
Foreword by: Kersi Meher-Homji

To my wife Anisha, without whose unwavering belief and continuing encouragement, I would never have started writing again

Contents

Contents   4

Introduction   6

Foreword –by *Kersi Meher-Homji*   9

KS Ranjitsinhji: The Maharaja of Elegance   12

A Messerschmitt up your arse and other War Stories   21

The Award for the Worst Declaration in history   36

In Melbourne, Bradman did the unexpected   43

Butterfingers: Dropped catches and other tales   47

The five best bowling performances in cricket history   52

Have fat, can bat   61

The summer of '48 and two of the greatest wicketkeepers   65

When West Indies met their Waterloo in Ireland   79

A tale of two debuts: The Banerjee-Warne story   86

Head and shoulders above the rest   92

Meltdown at the death: It is just not cricket   99

The Invincibles on my wall: The 1948 Australian team sheet   105

The Last Word   114

Appendix – The Scorecards   116

Introduction

"Cricket was my reason for living" – Harold Larwood

Sometimes as you go through life doing what the world expects you to do and meet the challenges it throws at you along the way, you forget what it is that you really love doing. Such was the case with me.

Writing and Cricket, my two enduring loves, would stay forever on the backburner of life. Or so it seemed.

For the better part of two decades I built a successful career in banking, moving back and forth across the seven seas. A career that started in in the early 1990s in New Delhi, then took me to Kolkata and finally Mumbai. The start of the Noughties took me to Hong Kong for a few years, then back to Mumbai, then back to Hong Kong, onwards to London and then on to Singapore.

I had given up playing cricket on medical advice a few years ago, but could not let go of my deep passion for the game. If I could not play the game, I could surely follow it vicariously through Television and Social Media. And so there started the interaction with a group of like-minded cricket fanatics, who cloaked their single-minded obsession with the game by calling themselves the '*Sports Crazies*'.

For hours, nay for days, we would argue endlessly about every aspect of cricket – its present, its past and indeed its future. Friendships sprung up, which sometimes resulted in meetings but more often remained on social media.

A couple of years ago, after several heated exchanges with fellow group members, I decided to write an opinion piece on cricket on an issue I felt strongly about. My intent was to post it in the group, but on an impulse, I sent it off to an Australian website 'The Roar' where a fellow 'Crazy', Ritesh Misra, had just published an article.

The next morning, much to my surprise, The Roar had carried the article. What was most gratifying was the response of the readers of Roar. There was disagreement with my views certainly from some, but wide praise for the writing from most. Equally overwhelming was the support from fellow 'Crazies', which has remained unstinting over this period.

To Ritesh and the 'Sports Crazies' must go the credit of breaking the shell around my creativity.

A major turning point on this journey was an email that I received from Kersi Meher-Homji, one of the world's great Cricket Historians and the author of 14 books on Cricket. Kersi read one of my articles on The Roar and wrote in to say how much he had enjoyed it. He also encouraged me to keep writing. His encouragement was the water my creative tree needed.

My romance with Cricket Writing was in bloom.

In the past couple of years, I have been writing extensively on the history of cricket, delving into the past, to discover the romance of matches played and the quirkiness of the characters that made the game what it is. It has become a mission with me to help uncover the deeds of forgotten cricketing heroes and bring to life long forgotten stories from cricketing fields around the world, from Melbourne to Ireland, from Kolkata to Philadelphia.

It is with great pleasure that I bring together a small collection of my writing that has been published in the past couple of years on various platforms around the world, including The Roar, Cricket Country and *ESPN Cricinfo* to name just three. I have also had thought pieces published in India's iconic sports journal, *Sportstar* and the regional publication from Odisha, *Pragativadi*.

I must make special mention of the editorial teams at *The Roar* and *Cricket Country*, which have been particularly supportive on this continuing and exciting journey.

An important part of the reader experience is now my blog where my writing and other cricket writing that I recommend can be found. www.cricketwriter.com 'The Cricket Writer Weekend Quiz' has now become a staple diet for those who follow my writing!

I hope you enjoy the eclectic collection of articles you will find here. Hopefully it whets your appetite for my forthcoming book '*Spell-binding Spells*', which will be released this autumn.

Foreword

By Kersi Meher-Homji

These days, cricket literature has become a retired Test cricketer's domain. Most best-sellers are either autobiographies or biographies of Test greats. Over ninety percent of television commentators are former Test players.

Cricket writing with few exceptions has become less stimulating in this decade. We can't go back to the days of Neville Cardus, RC Robertson-Glasgow, John Arlott, EW Swanton, AA Thomson, Ray Robinson, CLR James, KN Prabhu and Jack Fingleton.

Peter Roebuck held the flag for top quality journalism until tragedy struck in 2011. Among modern cricket writers John Woodcock, David Frith, Mike Coward and Scyld Berry are near retirement.

I was bemoaning this last year when I read an article by a new name on *The Roar*, an Australian sports website. It was on spell-binding bowling spells in Test cricket by Anindya Dutta and I was impressed. Wow, this is something different as the article combined history, statistics and sheer excitement.

I was moved to write a comment on this story and we started corresponding on-line. Anindya Dutta is an Indian living in Singapore and a banker by profession. In the last few months I have read many of his sports stories on different websites with increasing interest.

I feel privileged to write a Foreword for his book A Gentleman's Game – Reflections on Cricket History. I enjoyed reading this well-illustrated and many-splendoured publication. Each Chapter starts with a famous quote.

The first Chapter is on "Ranjitsinhji, the Maharaja of Elegance and of Nawanagar". My initial reaction was: what is there on Ranji a cricket-lover does not know about? But after reading Anindya's book I learnt many things about Ranji I did not know. Some of it was not pleasant. In the beginning of his career there was a racist article on him written by Sir Home Gordon who called him "a dirty black". And did you know Ranji faced bankruptcy and earlier on he had no right to call himself a Prince?

The Chapter on Keith Miller – the supreme all-round cricket icon, a war hero, a classical music aficionado and a lovable character – starts with his immortal quote: "Pressure? There is no pressure in Test cricket. Real pressure is when you are flying a Mosquito with a Messerschmitt up your arse." Apart from his heroics on the cricket field author Anindya depicts Miller's courage and gallantry during World War II.

The author also mentions unsung war veterans and cricketers Graham Williams, Lionel Tennyson, Bob Crisp among others.

Being a quirky cricket writer myself I found Chapters on fattest and tallest cricketers fascinating. The research on bulky cricketers is aptly titled "Have Fat, Can Bat: Cricketers who were their weight in gold." Who were they? I won't tell you; you will have to read the book.

The book is not just about achievements. It details failures too: the worst declarations in history and on dropped catches by butterfingers. Also the mighty West Indies lost a match to Ireland. At one stage the Windies under Clive Lloyd were 8 for 6, 12 for 8 before being bowled out for 25. A misprint? A joke? No, it happened.

I found the Chapter "A Tale of Two Test Debuts" nostalgic as I was present at the Sydney Cricket Ground when Australia's Shane Warne and India's Subroto Banerjee had made their Test debuts in

January 1992. Medium-pacer Banerjee captured 3 for 47 including the scalps of Geoff Marsh, Mark Taylor and Mark Waugh. In contrast Warne had a forgettable debut, being smashed all over the park by Ravi Shastri and Sachin Tendulkar as he finished with 1 for 150.

Warne became a Test legend with 708 wickets at 25.41 in 145 Tests. For Banerjee it was his Test debut and swan song as he was never selected in a Test again.

To quote Anindya Dutta, "*Bizarrely, the man who has bowled so well in the first innings, Subroto Banerjee, does not get to bowl a single ball in the second innings. In fact, he never gets to bowl another ball in Test cricket, and is destined to be forever referred to in cricketing history as a one-Test wonder.*" Cricket cruel cricket!

Thus *A Gentleman's Game – Reflections on Cricket History* shows many aspects of cricket; the good, the gallant and the paradoxical. I enjoyed reading it. So will you.

KS Ranjitsinhji: The Maharaja of Elegance — and of Nawanagar

"Find out where the ball is, get there; hit it." – KS Ranjitsinhji

Images: Ranji playing the Leg Glance and as Jam Sahib

Neville Cardus, who, to those of us that in our own humble ways seek to follow in his enormous footsteps, was more a cricket poet than a cricket writer, described KS Ranjitsinhji thus: *"when Ranji batted a strange light was seen for the first time on English fields, a light out of the East."*

For Cardus, there was far more to Ranji than his leg-glance, something almost mystical in the way that he played his game, indeed in the way he approached the game.

But then that was Cardus the writer, about whom Arunabha Sengupta , writing in *Cricket Country*, very eloquently said: "*For Cardus, cricket was a muse — honest men plying their trade took on the stature of mythical luminaries, and often commonplace deeds were presented as eternal quests. The facts often fell prey, burnt down by the brilliant fireworks of wordplay. Cardus converted cricket reporting to literature in the form of historical fiction, which seldom gave credence to accuracy over art. Treating him as historian would be falling victim to a spectacular illusion.*"

Nonetheless, in the case of Ranji, Cardus was right.

In an age when wickets and heads were uncovered, spinners like Hugh Trumble often opened bowling on sticky wickets making the ball bite, turn and take off with spite and venom, and some of the greatest batsmen to ever stride the 22-yards, like WG Grace and Victor Trumper, were scoring all their runs on the offside, Ranji, single-handedly, pioneered the leg-side game.

Over three glorious days of an English summer in 1896, at Old Trafford, Ranji scored 62 and 154, with a majority of his runs coming on the leg-side, through a stroke that would quaintly be named the '*glance*'.

Though the leg-glance was not Ranji's invention, it was still a rarity. How utterly revolutionary this was at the time is attested to by Ranji's close friend CB Fry, no mean batsman himself, who recounted what he was told as a schoolboy: "*If one hit the ball in an unexpected direction on the on side, intentionally or otherwise, one apologised to the bowler... The opposing captain never, by any chance, put a fieldsman there; he expected you to drive on the off side like a gentleman.*"

But the leg-glance was not all there was to Ranji's batting.

With his wonderful hand-eye coordination, Ranji was able to go on the back foot and defend the ball, something no one before him had dared to attempt. About his preference for back-foot play, Ranji explains in his seminal work, *The Jubilee Book of Cricket*, "*It is impossible for forward play to be quite as safe as back play, because there must be a moment when the ball is out of sight ... On a treacherous wicket all the batsman can do is to watch the ball with all his might and let the bat follow the eye.*"

And clearly in line with this observation, when the ball had passed him on the offside, he would execute a stroke that could only ever be described as a '*late cut*', leaving the outstretched gloves of the bewildered wicketkeeper grasping at empty air.

Simon Wilde, one of his biographers, wrote about Ranji: "*The crowds would stroll the outfield during intervals in play ... at a loss to explain what he did: the most disdainful flick of the wrists, and he could exasperate some of England's finest bowlers; the most rapid sweep of the arms, and the ball was charmed to any part of the field he chose, as though he had in his hands not a bat but a wizard's wand."*

Ranji made his First-Class debut for Sussex at Lord's in 1895 with scores of 77 and 150 against MCC (he added 6 wickets and a couple of catches for good measure). That season he scored 1,766 runs at an average of 50.16 and finished third in the First-Class averages. Ranji was to score more than 1,000 runs in 10 successive seasons including more than 3,000 in both 1899 and 1900.

Ranji led Sussex for six years between 1898 and 1903 and then returned to India. He was to play two more complete seasons in 1908 and 1912, and in both he scored over 1,000 runs. In the one overseas trip to Australia that Ranji undertook in 1897-98, he scored 1,157 runs at 60.89.

Overall, for the times, considering he was not born in England, and his debut for England was vehemently opposed on that ground by MCC President Lord Harris, who had an intense dislike for Indians, Ranji had an impressive Test record.

In fact, despite his supreme debut effort at Old Trafford when he scored the 62 and 154 not out, his selection for the rest of the Ashes series was debated at Lord's. Writing in *Background of Cricket*, Sir Home Gordon was to recall: *"Old gentlemen waxing plethoric declared that if England could not win without resorting to the assistance of coloured individuals of Asiatic extraction, it had better devote its skill to marbles. Feelings grew so acrimonious as to sever lifelong friendships… one veteran told me that if it were possible he would have me expelled from MCC for having 'the disgusting degeneracy to praise a dirty black'."*

Notwithstanding the initial opposition, in a career spanning 6-years, Ranji played 15 Tests, all against Australia, scoring almost 1,000 runs at an average of 44.95 with 2 centuries and 6 fifties.

His First-Class record was even more remarkable. He played 307 matches over a career spanning 27 years (he played his last First-Class fixture when he was 48), scoring 24,692 runs at an average of 56.37 with 72 centuries and a high score of 285 not out.

And to what did he owe this phenomenal success?

CB Fry, talking about Ranji's strengths, provides a perspective: *"He tries to make every stroke a thing of beauty itself, and he does mean so well by the ball while he is in. He starts with one or two enormous advantages, which he has pressed home. He has a wonderful power of sight which enables him to judge the flight of a ball in the air an appreciable fraction of a second sooner than any other batsman, and probably a trifle more accurately. He can therefore decide in better time what stroke is wanted, and can make sure of getting into the right position to make it."*

It is worthwhile to look at Ranji's personal life, which was inextricably linked, and in no small measure defined Ranji the cricketer. It was also ultimately responsible for cutting short his career as a Test player.

Kumar Shri Ranjitsinhji, the second son of a minor nobleman Jiwansinghji, was born in the small town of Sarodar in the Indian province of Kathiawar. The local ruler of the province, Jam Sahib Vibhaji, did not have any male children, and Ranji was selected as the heir apparent.

But the story goes that discouraged by the ambition of Ranji's family and the conduct of Jiwansinhji, Vibhaji never completed the adoption of Ranjitsinhji. In 1882, one of the women of Vibhaji's court gave birth to a son, Jaswantsinhji. Even though Ranjitsinhji was no longer heir, Vibhaji continued to finance him and give him an allowance.

At Cambridge, Ranji adopted the title Prince Ranjitsinhji, although he had no right to call himself a Prince. However, he increasingly lived beyond his means to the point where he experienced financial difficulty. Eventually, Ranji was unable to appear for the Bar exam, having spent all his money on his lifestyle, and left Cambridge without a degree, but armed with a Cambridge Blue in cricket.

In 1896 Vibhaji died, his 12-year-old son Jaswantsinhji officially succeeded to the throne taking the new name Jassaji. With the throne beyond him in any event, Ranji concentrated on his cricket and 1896 and 1897 were excellent seasons for him and he was firmly established in the England team.

By 1898, buoyed by his rising popularity in England and India, Ranji decided to go to India and challenge Jassaji's succession. While his efforts did not bear the fruit he wished for, on this trip he did meet his next benefactor, Rajinder Singh, the Maharaja of Patiala, a huge cricket fan, who was to support Ranji's lifestyle for the next three years.

And then came November 1900, and the untimely passing of Rajinder Singh.

Ranji's life descended into chaos. Within a year he was facing bankruptcy. He travelled to India to address the situation and secure financial support. Not only was this a fruitless endeavour, but it caused him to miss the start of the 1902 season. Ranji returned in mid-May to captain Sussex, but he was woefully out of form.

But when the 1902 series against the visiting Australians started, Ranji was picked for the first Test. By this time, it was unthinkable that an English batting line up would not show his name, so popular and dominating had Ranji become in the cricketing firmament.

Ranji struggled with his form from the start, and had a nightmarish start running out his captain Archie MacLaren. *Wisden* described the incident as "*a misunderstanding, for which Ranjitsinhji considered himself somewhat unjustly blamed, led to MacLaren being run out, and then Ranjitsinhji himself quite upset by what had happened, was clean bowled*". Ranji had scored 13.

That would turn out to be his highest score of the series.

He did not bat in the second innings, played in the second Test that lasted for all of 105 minutes before being washed out. This gave just enough time for Ranji to be bowled off his pad by Bert Hopkins for a duck, attempting a leg-glance without getting his eye set. He did not play the third Test, making himself unavailable citing injury.

When the fourth Test started, the wicket was playing well and Victor Trumper scored a magnificent 104 to take Australia to 299. Luck was not with England, as it rained overnight, and with the sun out the next morning, and the wicket drying, it was a tailor-made situation for Hugh Trumble, opening the bowling. As *Wisden* described it, "*The wicket had been drying fast since luncheon and the Englishmen on going in to bat could do little or nothing against Trumble and Saunders, five wickets going down in three-quarters of an hour for 44.*"

Ranji, alas, was one of them, going back to a Trumble delivery that thudded into his pads, when he had scored 2. Things did not improve for Ranji in the second innings, when he departed with his score at 4, dismissed in identical fashion to the same bowler.

Ranji was then dropped for the fifth Test, having scored a total of 19 runs in the 4 innings he batted in that series.

That was the last time Ranji would play Test cricket for England.

Years later, writing about the ironies of careers of cricketers, Cardus would wistfully say in *The Cricketer*, "*In 1902, Ranjitsinhji, second in the First-Class averages, scored 19 runs in four completed innings against Australia, such an eclipse of genius which the game had never known before and has not known since.*"

And despite Cardus' hyperbolic assertion that "*when Ranji passed out of cricket a wonder and a glory departed from the game forever*", the genius and personality of Ranji and the long-term impact of his contribution to the game, ensures that his name shines as brightly today as it did that 17th day of July in 1896.

Ranji would eventually become the Maharaja Jam Sahib of Nawanagar when Jassaji died of a mysterious illness for which no aspersions were cast on possible beneficiaries, although certain questions were raised.

This article was originally published in 'Cricket Country' on April 28, 2017.

A Messerschmitt up your arse and other War Stories

"Pressure? There is no pressure in Test cricket. Real pressure is when you are flying a Mosquito with a Messerschmitt up your arse."

— Keith Miller

Images: Keith Miller and Cyril Lowe

"Pressure? There is no pressure in Test cricket. Real pressure is when you are flying a Mosquito with a Messerschmitt up your arse."

That, dear readers, was Keith Miller, answering a question from Michael Parkinson before one of the Victory Tests played after World War II.

Keith Miller, cricketer, nay personality extraordinaire.

Swashbuckling cricketer, daring fighter pilot, debonair looks put to full romantic effect, and a lover of classical music such that it once prompted him to turn his Mosquito back into the war zone so he could take a detour of Bonn, Beethoven's birthplace.

His love of music once got him into even greater trouble. He went AWOL to watch violinist Yehudi Menuhin perform in London and was dismissed, but the CO revoked his decision on the condition that Miller play for his cricket team.

A man always ready to offer perspective. A man who lived life king size, reportedly having a torrid affair with Princess Margaret at one time, but a man who was also a truly caring human being.

Ashley Mallett once wrote about a wartime episode of Miller's: "*For much of the war, Miller was based near Bournemouth. Every Friday night it became tradition for Miller and his mates from the RAF base to meet at the Carlton Hotel in Bournemouth. One fateful Friday night, Miller couldn't make the regular appointment and when he returned he found the town barricaded after a German raid. A Focke-Wulf fighter bomber had strafed the church next to the hotel, causing the church spire to collapse directly on to the front bar, instantly killing his eight mates. Each year for more than 50 years*

Miller returned to England and spent time with a relative of each of his mates killed that tragic night in 1943."

But Miller wasn't the only one.

Sport has a way of finding characters whose impact goes well beyond the playing fields, and touches the core of what life means. War, and its experiences, unfortunately has sometimes played more than its fair share of a role in shaping such men.

And while this is not merely a Keith Miller journey, he is however an important character in our next story.

The year was 1945, the war had just ended in Europe, and everyone was looking for ways to get back to normal life quickly. In this scenario, a series of 5 First-Class matches, called the Victory Tests (the Australian Board refused to accept them as official Tests) were played between the Australian Services XI and England, and the teams met for the first of the three-day matches at Lord's on May 19, 1945.

England had Wally Hammond, now 42, but still a giant of the game, as well as Len Hutton, Cyril Washbrook and Bill Edrich, all freed from active service. Denis Compton was still serving in the Far East and Hedley Verity had sadly not survived the war.

Australia was without Don Bradman, who had been invalidated out of the war due to 'Fibrositis', a painful muscle spasm condition affecting his back, and only had the services of Australian servicemen still in Britain.

But players like spinner Reg Ellis and batsman Ross Stanford, who had been the RAAF's leading batsman in England between flying Lancaster sorties over Germany, were getting their chance to represent their country. And then there was Miller, who had rushed over after finishing his last sortie over Germany, with a few days break spent relaxing in gentler company.

But the most poignant moment of the match came when Australian airman Graham Williams walked out to bat at No. 9 with Miller batting on hundred at the other end.

In an interview years later, Miller was to recall the scene: *"He was given a great ovation that compares with anything ever given Bradman, Lillee or Richards. But it was not the sort of clapping and cheering that greets a hundred. This is different. Everyone stood up. They all knew about Graham's captivity. He was a big fella, but he was gaunt from his experience, and he just walked round for a while as if in a trance."*

He then went to say, *"It was almost orchestral in its sound and feeling. Whenever I think of it, tears still come to my eyes."*

Two weeks before this match, Williams had been freed from a German POW camp after 4-years of captivity. He had been captured early in the war when his plane crashed in the Middle East, and had survived on starvation rations. He was 31 kg below his pre-War bodyweight, when he walked out to the middle at Lord's.

He was so weak that he had to be given glucose between overs.

He was to score 53 runs at a-run-a-ball and take 2 wickets bowling 40 overs in that first match.

After the Victory Tests, Williams never played First-Class cricket again. He received an MBE for his commitment to teaching blind prisoners Braille during the war, which he had done through the 4-years of captivity. Williams passed away at the age of 67 in 1978.

A picture of the Australian Services Team walking out to field in the first Victory Test, with a tall gaunt Williams bringing up the rear on the extreme left of the photo, was always the one which adorned the best wall in Miller's home for as long as he lived. He called it the most memorable moment of his life.

In a life as colourful and accomplished as Miller's, that was quite a statement.

When the First World War (or 'Great War', as it was called at the time) broke out and England joined on August 4, 1914, First-Class Cricket continued to be played for a few weeks until WG Grace wrote to *The Sportsman* encouraging cricketers to enlist: "*The time has arrived when the county cricket season should be closed. It is not fitting at a time like this that able-bodied men should be playing day after day, and pleasure seekers look on. There are so many who are young and able, and still hanging back. I should like to see all first-class cricketers of suitable age set a good example, and come to the aid of their country without delay in its hour of need.*"

Heeding this call and perhaps feeling the patriotic urge in any case, 210 of the 278 professional cricketers registered in England, enlisted for the war. By the end of the war, nearly a sixth of them were dead, and at one stage, *Wisden* was printing obituaries in the space reserved for match reports.

One of those who enlisted was Lionel Tennyson, the 24-year old grandson of Lord Alfred Tennyson, having just returned from a successful tour of South Africa in March 1914 as a part of the last pre-war England Cricket Team.

In the best traditions of the family, he kept written records of his experiences which he later penned in *Diary of the Great European War*.

Despatched to Le Havre with the Rifle Brigade in August 1914, he wrote: "*Told to march downhill at once to the station and push off to the front as fast as we could. The English had had a severe defeat and heavy casualties and we were wanted in the firing line as soon as possible.*"

He was to remain on or near the front lines for the next four years, and experience all the horrors of war his grandfather so eloquently described in his *Charge of the Light Brigade*. He was wounded thrice and twice mentioned in the despatches for his gallant or meritorious action in the face of the enemy.

In his 1933 autobiography *From Verse to Worse*, Tennyson was to recount his return to the front from his second war-wound thus: "*I *have never liked travelling light and so, though the amount of kit I arrived with may, in fact have aroused a certain amount of astonishment, I was quickly forgiven by my commanding officer as well as by everyone else, when they found out that it included, among other things, a case of champagne."*

More sombrely, and no less eloquently than his grandfather, the younger Tennyson was to write of his war experiences, *"The bits of men, clothes, rifles etc. in the trenches, men dead and dying, are better left unthought of."*

Unlike Major Booth (who caused some confusion in the Yorkshire regiment to which he was assigned given the fact that he was actually a Second Lieutenant) and Colin Blythe, both teammates from that pre-War England team, Tennyson was to survive the war, and despite being left with one good hand, was to go on and captain the England Test team.

Tennyson captained Hampshire from 1919 to 1932. In 1921, after England lost 6 successive Tests to the Australians led by Warwick Armstrong, he was recalled to the England side for the second Test, which England lost. But Tennyson scored a gritty 74 in the second innings against Jack Gregory and Ted McDonald at their fastest.

In no small measure for the grit he showed, he was appointed captain for the remaining three matches of that series. That was the high point in Tennyson's career, as indeed it would have been for anyone given the ultimate honour of captaining one's country.

English and Australian cricketers were however not the only ones whose careers and lives were impacted by the wars.

Pieter van der Bijl of South Africa, a very large man, made his first sporting mark in college as a heavyweight boxer. And as EW Swanton was to write in his obituary for *The Cricketer* many years later, he "*was a cricketer who surprised his friends, and undoubtedly himself, by playing with distinction for his country after a modest University career.*"

Slow-footed by nature but hugely courageous and often dour in his approach, van der Bijl was selected to make his debut in the first Test of the 1938-39 series. He distinguished himself with scores of 125 and 97 in the famous "*Timeless Test*" at Durban, which, despite the best effort of both teams for a result, had to be abandoned as a draw on the 10th playing day, when England were 42 runs away from what would have been an astonishing fourth-innings winning total of 696.

Pouring rain, and England's necessary departure to catch the mailship they were booked on for the passage back home, ensured the match could not carry on, and Hammond's offer of a draw was gratefully accepted.

In his innings of 125, van der Bijl took 45 minutes to get off the mark and five hours to complete his century, but between his dour defence on and outside the off-stump, the big man did have one exceptional over off Doug Wright when he scored 22 runs with 5 fours.

Those 5 Tests were, however, all van der Bijl was to play in his career. Despite a batting average of 51, the onset of the war ensured the end of his career.

He signed up for the army and distinguished himself fighting in North Africa. In 1942, he took the decision to run his jeep out under fire to bring back half-a-dozen men lying wounded in the heat.

He saved the lives of the men but was severely wounded himself, and would never wear cricketing flannels again.

Pieter van der Bijl devoted himself to teaching, and for a brief period was a South African Test selector.

His son Vintcent van der Bijl was perhaps the best South African fast bowler never to have played for his country because of the ban for apartheid.

Pieter van Der Bijl passed away in 1973 at the age of 65.

And then there was Bob Crisp, a South African cricketer born in Calcutta, about whose life Gideon Haigh said, "*Many lives in one, all of them worth living*", and Andy Bull, in *The Guardian*, labelled "*the most extraordinary man to play Test cricket.*"

So what was it about Crisp that was so special?

Crisp is the only Test cricketer to have climbed Mount Kilimanjaro twice. One of the stories that have gone into folklore is about Crisp climbing Kilimanjaro when South Africa announced their squad for a Test series with England.

On his way back, near the foothills, he met a friend who had never climbed the peak. On hearing this, he made up his mind to climb the peak again, this time with his friend in tow. When they had almost made it, his friend broke his leg; so Crisp carried him up and then all the way down.

Crisp played 62 First-Class matches, taking 276 wickets at 19.88. He remains the only bowler to take four wickets in four balls twice in First-Class cricket. Nine of these First-Class matches were Tests for a weak South African side, in which he captured 20 wickets at 37.35 — all within one year.

Andy Bull wrote: "*Crisp was a fast bowler, who had the knack of making the ball bounce steeply and, when the weather suited, swing both ways.*" One imagines, in the days of scantily covered pitches, he was quite a handful in the course of his relatively short career.

But then, like the rest of our heroes, Bob Crisp went to war.

Ben Thompson, in his weekly blog *Badass of the Week*, summed up Crisp's war years thus: "*During the action in the Balkans, Bob Crisp managed to have three tanks (tanks!) shot out from under him (he bailed out and survived with minor burns/shrapnel wounds all three times), fired a .38-caliber revolver at a German Mark IV Panzer on more than one occasion, blasted a dozen enemy tanks, and miraculously shot down a twin-engine Henkel Bomber with a cupola-mounted .50-caliber Browning machine gun right as it was about to make a bombing run on a British Armoured Column."*

Crisp described his own elevation within three short months to Captain and Tank Commander far more modestly: "*I owed this entirely to the fact that I played cricket for South Africa and my commanding officer had once played county cricket for Hampshire.*"

Crisp's luck, however, was too good to last forever and he was hit by shrapnel in the skull while commanding his tank in the desert.

Crisp recounted years later: "*My knees started to buckle under immediately and, at the same time, I knew I had been hit in the head. My first emotion was astonishment. Almost coincident with the explosion was this feeling of great surprise: 'I've been hit. Well. I'm damned.' It was a few minutes before I went unconscious. I was only out for 20 minutes. From the first impact I had felt no pain at all. Yet my skull had been fractured, a piece of metal was touching the brain, and half my ear had been torn off. I spent six hours, conscious, in the bottom of that tank before they could get me out, but the agony came not from my head but from my legs. They were crunched up awkwardly underneath me without circulation, and I was too heavy and the space too confined for anybody to move me. It was excruciating.*"

And that was the end of Crisp's war. Given his injuries, he never bowled again.

This did not however prevent him leading an incredibly colourful post war life supported by his work as a journalist. That is a story well told by Andy Bull and Abhishek Mukherjee in their respective articles on this incredible cricketer and war hero, and well worth a read!

The fine line and deep connect between sporting courage and personal valour does not, however, belong exclusively to the game of cricket. The onset of the World Wars meant that all sport and the men and women who played them, were impacted.

The case of England Rugby International and First World War flying ace, Cyril Lowe is a case in point.

Cyril Lowe was a diminutive 5ft 6in and at 50kg a relative lightweight, but with immense courage and tremendous speed, off and on the rugby field. His favourite statement through his life was, *"If you set your mind to do something, you can do anything"*. He won 25 consecutive caps, scored 18 tries on the wing and brought home 4 Grand Slams. His first Grand Slam was in 1914 and the fourth in 1923.

Between his trophies, he fought a war.

As a RAF ace, he saved numerous lives through his quick reactions, and had a significant number of successes in the air. Once he brought down nine German planes, but was wounded and his plane caught fire. Those were the days when parachutes existed but were not allowed because, hold your breath, "*the presence of such an apparatus might impair the fighting spirit of pilots.*"

Lowe used every bit of his skill and survival instinct to get safely back over the lines and survived the ensuing crash.

Or take the incredible story of Irish Rugby player Blair 'Paddy' Mayne. As Brough Scott, writing in *The Telegraph* in the early part of this century, would narrate: "*Mayne, who had been the star of the Lions' 1938 South African tour, was a quietly spoken, poetry-reading lawyer until he was roused.*"

He first saw action in June 1941 as a lieutenant with 11 Commando during the Syria–Lebanon Campaign. Mayne successfully led his men during the Litani River Operation in Lebanon against Vichy French Forces.

His leadership on the raid had attracted the attention of Captain David Stirling who recruited him as one of the early members of the Special Air Service (SAS).

As Major, Mayne was appointed to command the Special Raiding Squadron and led the unit in Sicily and Italy until the end of 1943. In Sicily, Mayne was awarded a bar to his DSO. In January 1944 he was promoted to Lieutenant-Colonel and appointed Commanding Officer of the re-formed 1st SAS Regiment. He subsequently led the SAS with great distinction through the final campaigns of the war in France, the Netherlands, Belgium, Germany and Norway.

During the course of the War he became one of the British Army's most highly decorated soldiers and received the DSO with three bars, one of only seven British servicemen to receive that award four times during World War 2. Additionally, the post-War French Government awarded him the Legion d'honneur and the Croix de Guerre.

Just the narration of even one episode of his war years is sufficient to explain why he was such a decorated hero.

One of his men was killed in an ambush near Poppberg, North-West Germany, in March 1945. Mayne, the poet, not easily roused, was roused now.

He got the others out of the jeep and took a Bren and a Tommy Gun. Then he drove flat out at the Germans' house, kicked the door in and literally shot everyone inside. For speed, daring, effect and ruthlessness there has seldom been anything to match it in any field of war, much less in a sporting arena.

Tragically for the sport in Ireland, his daring exploits during the War were to leave Mayne with permanent damage to his back. He worked as a solicitor on his return to Ireland, but the severe back pain that was now chronic, would never again allow him back to the rugby field, not even as spectator.

The sad truth of the matter is that long as there are humans on this earth, we shall fight each other, on the playing fields, and on the battle fields.

So while we rejoice in the sporting victories of our heroes in peace time, let us spare a moment or two of thought for those heroes like Verity and thousands of others who conquered the sporting fields only to perish in the killing fields.

And those, like the Millers, Tennysons, Lowes and Maynes, who came back heroes of another kind, in many cases, to carry on where they had left off, as if nothing had changed.

But of course, everything had changed.

As the bomb that fell on Lord's in 1941 showed, the line between the playing field and the killing field had just blurred.

A lesson in history we would do well to remember.

This article was originally published in 'Cricket Country' on March 14, 2017.

The Award for the Worst Declaration in history

"Any captain can only do his best for the team and for cricket. When you are winning, you are a hero. Lose, and the backslappers fade away." – Richie Benaud

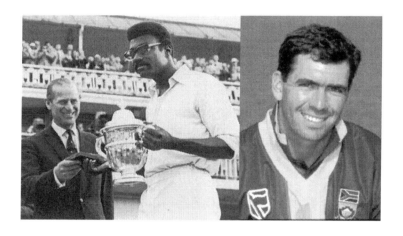

Images: Clive Lloyd and Hansie Cronje

In cricket, a challenging declaration in the second innings is about as close as a captain ever gets to taking a gamble on the field.

The opportunity cost of not being able to score more runs is pretty hard to swallow, so it's not surprising that declarations are a not a frequent occurrence.

Nor is it surprising that some have gone spectacularly wrong.

January 10, 1935: Bridgetown

On a rain-affected pitch in the first Test of the 1934-35 series, England dismisses the West Indies for a modest total of 102, despite a gritty two-hour knock of 44 by George Headley against some hostile pace and spin on a wet wicket. England goes into bat, and despite resistance from Wally Hammond, at the end of the first day is precariously placed at 5-81.

Then it rains so much that play restarts only at tea on Day 3. As soon as England comes into bat, they lost two wickets, and captain RES Wyatt declares the innings closed at 7-81.

From being 3-4 at the start, the West Indies recovers to 3-33 at close of play.

And then it rains again.

Play restarts at 3pm on the fourth day, the sun shines brightly, and the wicket becomes even more difficult to negotiate.

The Windies get to 6-51 by tea, and at the interval, captain GC Grant decides to declare with a lead of 73, and push for a win on an unplayable pitch.

But, difficult as the pitch is, Hammond realises that if he can be stodgy in defence, and play long enough, England can win this. And so they do, with Hammond driving a huge six to bring up a most unlikely victory.

37

It is the first adverse result of a third innings declaration in Test cricket.

July 27th, 1948: Leeds

England and Australia meet at Leeds for the fourth Test of the first post-war Ashes series played in England, in what would turn out to be a remarkable match. A rejuvenated 40-year-old Don Bradman leads an Australian team that will later earn the sobriquet of '*The Invincibles*', eager to achieve a 4-0 sweep.

On a perfect wicket, England wins the toss, bats first, and scores a mammoth 496. Australia replies with 458, scored at a much faster pace. England again bats extremely well in the second innings, and captain Norman Yardley decides that a target of 404 with 345 minutes on the last day is enough to put pressure on Australia and take a few quick wickets with the heavy roller breaking up the pitch.

Things don't quite turn out that way however.

The pitch breaks up, and the ball turns awkwardly and lifts. Bradman receives three reprieves from the Englishmen to remain not out on 173 and leads Australia to a famous victory.

For the first time in cricket history, a country has scored over 400 runs in the last innings to win a Test match. But it won't be the last.

In the 126 years since the first known declaration in cricket (Nottinghamshire declared at 5-157 against Kent in 1890), there have been many such brave decisions, and some have paid off handsomely.

Some, not so much.

April 12th 1976. Port of Spain.
India meets the West Indies in the third Test at Trinidad, one down in the series.

West Indies wins the toss and elects to bat, but is soon reeling at 52 for 3 against the brilliantly unpredictable Chandrasekhar and his fast leg spinners. But Vivian Richards is in majestic form and on the back of his 177 runs, West Indies ends Day 1 at 320 for 5, Chandra taking all five wickets.

The next morning, however, the wily Bishan Bedi wraps up the West Indian innings in quick time for 359.

On a turning Port of Spain pitch, Lloyd believes that his three spinners will do more damage to the Indians than they inflicted on his batsmen. However it is actually the sole effort of Michael Holding that breaks the back of the Indian batting.

Bowling with great pace and aggression, Holding gets Gavaskar cheaply and then runs through the Indian attack over the next day or so, taking six wickets just as Chandra did in the previous innings, and India is all out for 228, a deficit of 131 runs.

Between Chandra and Venkat, the third member of India's spinning trio in that Test, the Indians make rapid inroads into the West Indies batting dismissing Richards and Clive Lloyd relatively cheaply.

Despite a tentative century from Kallicharan, the West Indies only gets to 271 for the loss of six wickets one hour after lunch on the fourth day and with a lead of 402 runs, Lloyd decides he has enough runs to dismiss the Indians cheaply with three spinners at his disposal on a broken track.

Two brothers-in-law batting for the Indian team, however, have other ideas.

Sunil Gavaskar and Gundappa Vishwanath, two of the smallest batsmen in Test cricket, score magnificent gritty centuries on a difficult pitch.

Mohinder Amarnath bats for 400 minutes to score 85, and a bearded Brijesh Patel comes in with the mandatory overs half done, and smashes the West Indian spinners all over the park to take India to a famous and unscripted victory.

It is the first time since 1948 when Bradman's Invincibles achieved the feat that a team has scored more than 400 to win in the fourth innings after a declaration by the opposition.

This loss however has a much bigger impact on the future of world cricket than people could imagine.

Lloyd is incensed at the impotence of his spinners on a turning track, and brings in a four-pacer attack for the final Test of the series to pound the Indians into submission.

It is the start of the West Indies pace quartet domination that is to rule cricket fields from Port of Spain to Eden Gardens for more than a decade.

January 18th 2000. Centurion.

This is a match that has gone down in history as the best example of something that appears to be too good to be true, and sure enough, it is.

South Africa comes into the fifth Test at Centurion having won the series 2-0 and with little to prove against the hapless English team.

South Africa struggles to 155 for 6 on a rain-curtailed first day. Then incessant rain means the next three days are washed out. So the obvious conclusion on Day 5 is that the Test will end in a tame draw.

Before play resumes however, South African captain Hansie Cronje bumps into Alec Stewart on the stairs and asks if Nassir Hussain would consider an offer to chase 270 in 73 overs to give England a chance to fight for a victory.

With South Africa up 2-0, it would not impact the result of the series, and the paying public would get something for their money. Hussain and Coach Fletcher decide to see how the first session goes before responding. When South Africa restarts play, the pitch plays true and Klusener and Pollock bat beautifully, and Darren Gough doesn't bowl well.

40 minutes into the day's play, Hussain decides to test Cronje by sending him a message asking whether South Africa would be willing to let England try and chase 250 instead. Much to his surprise, Cronje agrees, and in fact tells Hussain he can score 245 from 76 overs instead, an even better offer.

What happens next is pure Hollywood.

South Africa declares at 248 for 8. England then declares without playing a ball – the first time a team has ever declared at 0 for 0. South Africa then forfeits its innings, leaving England to score 249 runs to win the match.

England duly scores 251 for 8 to win the match. Michael Atherton describes the victory as *"the cheapest win of my Test career"*.

There is a lot of talk around the match, and while most of the media praises the arrangement, Derek Pringle, writing in *The Independent*, questions Cronje's motives, calling it an action out of character. On April 12th the same year, the fixing scandal breaks out, and three days later comes confirmation that Cronje was offered $150,000 by a bookie to be paid to a charity to ensure that the Centurion Test had a positive result.

The Centurion remains a black mark forever in Test cricket history, and a huge lesson to everyone that what looks too good to be true, usually is.

This article was originally published in two parts in 'The Roar' on September 22, 2016.

In Melbourne, 80 years ago, when captain Bradman did the unexpected

The game of cricket existed long before I was born. It will be played centuries after my demise. During my career I was privileged to give the public my interpretation of its character in the same way that a pianist might interpret the works of Beethoven.

- Sir Don Bradman

Image: Don Bradman and Stan McCabe walk out to bat

It is the third Ashes Test of the 1936-37 Series and the race for the greatest batsman in the world title is well and truly on between Donald Bradman and a certain Wally Hammond.

The first Test of the series at Brisbane had been a disaster for the normally prolific Bradman, scoring 38 and 0. Australia had lost by 322 runs. All out for 58 in the second innings was the icing on the cake for the English handing Australia a humiliating defeat.

The second Test at Sydney wasn't going much better when Wally Hammond scored 231 not out and England declared at 426 for 6 after a thunderstorm the third morning.

Bradman walked in and went for a first ball duck. Australia was all out for 80 on a "juiced up" pitch as a contemporary account had it.

Australia followed on and with Bradman on 24, Walter Robins dropped a hook from him that was going straight into his hands. It was going to be a costly miss.

In a precursor of a famous conversation that Steve Waugh and Herschelle Gibbs were said to be involved in a few decades later, Robin's captain Gubby Allen tells him *"Oh, don't give it a thought. You've just cost us the Ashes, that's all."*

Bradman went on to score 82 and was then bowled by Hedley Verity. Despite a gritty innings of 93 from Stan McCabe, England won the match by an innings and 22 runs.

Allen's comment turns out to be less prescient than Waugh's would be years later.

At that stage, Bradman's average from 4 innings was 30.

And the same question that Kersi Meher-Homji raised on *The Roar* this week about Steve Smith was being raised about Bradman — was his captaincy affecting his batting?

And then the teams came to Melbourne for the third Test.

A unique game of cricket was awaiting fans. Bradman called it "*a sensational battle of tactics as circumstances rarely allow.*"

As was the norm in those days, the pitch was uncovered. And it rained.

Australia bats first on a pitch that the Wisden Almanac called a "glue-pot" wicket. At 200 for 9, Bradman declares so that the Australian bowlers can get at England.

Sure enough, on an unplayable wicket, despite a brilliant 32 from Wally Hammond, England struggles to 76 for 9. Gubby Allen then declares, to in turn, get at the Aussie batsmen.

By then the sun is out, and Bradman plays an absolute masterstroke. Something no other captain has done until that point.

He sends in the Nos. 9, 10, and 11 to bat first up to give the top order a better chance on a sticky wicket that would hopefully have dried up by the time the main batsmen get to the middle.

His lower order batsmen do their best, and with Australia at 97 for 5, Bradman comes in to bat at No. 7.

He adds 346 for the sixth wicket with Jack Fingleton, Australia's opening batsman who has come in at No. 6. Bradman's aim is not only to score enough to win the game, but make a statement to the English team to tell them he is back.

The *Times of London* laments – "*Bradman's aim seems not only to kill the psychological advantage which England gained in the first second Test matches but to cremate it on a mammoth pyre of runs.*" Bradman scores 270 and leaves England an unattainable 689 runs to win the Test. England is bowled out for 323.

Bradman then scores a 212 in the fourth Test at Adelaide and a 169 in the final Test at Melbourne, amassing a mammoth 810 in the five matches to turn the series and give the Aussies a 3-2 Ashes victory.

The third Test 80 years ago in Melbourne had turned the series on its head, and Bradman's unconventional approach to captaincy, made this one of the most interesting Test matches in the history of cricket.

This article was originally published in 'The Roar' on November 12, 2016.

Butterfingers: Dropped catches and other tales from cricket history

"Pretend its Sunday, Reverend, and keep your hands together."

- Fred Trueman to David Sheppard

Images: Brian Lara raises bat after a ton and Len Hutton pulls

The Indian team has been lambasted for some pretty shoddy catching in the ongoing series against England.

And while better catching is highly desirable, this is hardly the first time a team has been *"contagiously bad"* in the catching department, as the archives amply demonstrate.

The Indian team, however, has had more than its fair share of this not so rare affliction.

In the second Test of the 1985 series in Colombo, India dropped seven catches against Sri Lanka on the first day, on which the only wicket to fall was thanks to a run-out.

India also dropped six catches in the space of ten overs in Rawalpindi in 2004, five of them coming in the first hour of the fourth day. It is rare enough for six chances to be offered at all in the space of ten overs, and it's absolutely criminal to drop all of them!

The ignominious record for most missed chances in a Test match for one team is 12, also held by India and achieved against England in Mumbai in 2006.

A couple of glorious individual mentions are also warranted about Indian cricketers, while we are about it!

The wicketkeeper with the most misses is MS Dhoni with 66 (18% of all catches offered to him).

In his defence, Dhoni had to deal with a high percentage of spin bowling, which presents a much greater challenge for keepers. Miss rates for leading wicketkeepers off spinners average around 30 per cent, and clearly Dhoni can be pardoned for this record.

Another interesting one is that the batsman with most reprieves is also an Indian – Virender Sehwag, missed 68 times, just one ahead of Sangakkara. About 37 per cent of the chances Sehwag offered were dropped, which is well above average and probably a testament to the power of his brutal hitting!

But India is far from being alone in the dropped catch record books.

The most missed chances in an innings are nine by Pakistan against England in Faisalabad in 2005, and also by Bangladesh against Pakistan in Dhaka in 2011.

And there have been some very expensive drops indeed in terms of runs scored thereafter by batsmen who were so reprieved.

In Karachi in 2009, when Sri Lanka played Pakistan, Mahela Jayawardene (240) was dropped on 17 and 43, Thilan Samaraweera (231) was dropped on 73 and 77, and Younis Khan (313) was dropped on 92. The combined cost of all the missed chances in that match was a staggering 1152 runs.

The best example from First Class cricket was the dropped catch of Brian Lara in 1994.

Lara had joined Warwickshire in the wake of his record 375 against England, and had already been bowled by a no-ball when he nicked one to Chris Scott, Durham's wicket keeper who dropped it. '*I suppose he'll get a hundred now,*' said Scott.

Not quite.

Lara finished with 501, still the highest ever first-class score.

Mark Taylor (334 not out) was dropped on 18 and 27 by Saeed Anwar, and there was a missed stumping on 40 for Len Hutton (364) in 1938.

Perhaps even luckier were Kumar Sangakkara, who made 270 in Bulawayo after being dropped on 0, and Sachin Tendulkar who was dropped on 0 when he made his highest score, 248 not out in Dhaka.

There was Inzamam-ul-Haq, who made 329 after being missed on 32 at Lahore in 2002, and Graham Gooch who was famously dropped by Kiran More when on 36 at Lord's in 1990. He went on to make 333.

The Ashes have a few stories to tell in this regard as well.

England and Australia went into the fourth Test at Headingley in 1997 tied at 1-1. After being dismissed for 172, England reduced Australia to 50 for three when debutant Mike Smith found the edge of Matthew Elliott's bat and the ball plopped gently into the hands of Graham Thorpe.

And then, as gently, it plopped out.

Elliott went on to make 199 and Australia won by an innings, then wrapped up the Ashes in the next Test. Smith finished wicket less, and never played for England again

Freddie Trueman was not famous for his subtlety when fielders dropped catches off his bowling. But there was no denying his sharp wit, as Rev. David Sheppard was to discover in the Sydney Test of the 1962-63 Ashes series.

Right after he had dropped a sitter at extra cover from Neil Harvey, one of a long series of catches that pretty much cost England the Ashes, an exasperated Trueman walked up to him and said, *"Pretend its Sunday, Reverend, and keep your hands together."*

And of course, no one who is reading this article, is likely to forget the most famous and expensive dropped catch of all.

Steve Waugh's supposed quip to Herschelle Gibbs in 1999 – "*You've just dropped the Word Cup, mate*", is immortal and just about the perfect line to end this piece!

This article was originally published in 'The Roar' on November 29, 2016.

The five best bowling performances in cricket history

"Such a fine chap and such a fine bowler."

– Frank Shipton on Hedley Verity

Images: Hedley Verity and Bert Vogler

Hedley Verity, George Geary, Premangshu Chatterjee, Bert Vogler and Albert Moss. I can see you shaking your heads at these names. Other than Verity, who has had a couple of excellent books written about his exploits, the other names are unlikely to ring any bells in the minds of most readers.

And yet, these fine men, forgotten largely by history as they are, hold the records for the best bowling figures in the history of First Class Cricket. Records that have stood the test of time, so much so, that the only performance that is even remotely modern dates back to 1957.

Hedley Verity 10-10

It is 1932, World War 2 is still seven years away, and peace reigns in an England whose wounds have barely healed from the loss of a generation of its young men in the great War.

Hedley Verity has just made his Test debut at the Oval against New Zealand the previous year, and will go on to earn fame as the man who dismissed Don Bradman more times than any other Test bowler, with his left arm spin.

He will also go on to form a close friendship with Douglas Jardine and Harold Larwood, whose example he had followed in making it out of the Coal pits into the bright sunshine of English cricket fields.

Verity would play 40 Tests for England in the intervening years, and take 144 wickets at 24.37 with a best performance of 8 for 43. He would finally earn immortality by passing away from his wounds as a prisoner of war in the country of his birth, Italy, in 1943, at the age of 38.

But we go back to 1932 when Yorkshire is playing Nottinghamshire at Leeds. Notts scores 234 in their first innings and Yorkshire replies with 163 for 9 before declaring on the third and final morning, in an effort to force a result. Notts takes the score to 44 for no loss, when Verity gets the ball.

In a remarkable collapse, Notts goes from 44 for no loss to 67 all out. In his first spell, Verity takes 3 wickets, and then in his second, he takes the other 7 in a jaw dropping 15-ball effort, including a hat-trick. His full figures are 19.4 overs, 16 maidens, 10 runs, 10 wickets.

It had rained the previous night, but that doesn't fully explain his achievement, because right after Notts is dismissed, Yorkshire opening batsmen Percy Holmes and Herbert Suttcliffe have an unbroken 139 run stand and take Yorks to a famous 10-wicket victory.

It is only fitting that 85 years later, we are still talking about this performance as being unmatched in its enormity.

George Geary 10-18
George Geary was the greatest cricketer Lancashire had produced until the advent of a certain David Gower.

But the closest parallel to bowling style that Geary had was a certain Aussie, who decades later, would become perhaps the greatest Australian fast bowler of all time – Glenn McGrath.

Contemporary accounts say: "*Because he was tall and very solidly built, he was able both to get bounce and to bowl the long spells required for success in Australian conditions which destroyed the reputations of all English bowlers of slighter build.*"

They also go on to say: "*Geary was able to swing the new ball very effectively but relied for most of his success on his amazing persistence and ability to bowl with slight yet well-disguised*

variations of pace and cut. He was able to bowl quite incredible
numbers of overs on unresponsive pitches."

Sounds familiar?

Unlike Verity however, Geary was a far more successful First Class
bowler than a Test performer, where he took 46 wickets at 29.41. In
First Class cricket, he took a staggering 2063 wickets at an
unbelievable 20 runs per wicket.

To witness his best bowling figures, however, we go back to 1929
when Glamorgan are playing Leicestershire at Pontypridd.

Leicester is bowled out for 102 with only three players reaching
double figures. Glamorgan, despite a fighting 70 from opener
William Bates, can only score 160, with Geary taking 6 for 78 in a
long 35-over spell.

Leicester does not do much better the second time and is bowled out
for 141, leaving Glamorgan an easy 84 runs to win the match. With a
day and a half left in the 3-day match, Leicester's players are already
packed, when they come out to bowl.

George Geary, however, has other ideas.

In a remarkable 16-over opening spell, he scythes through the
Glamorgan batting, and takes all 10 wickets giving away a measly
18 runs.

Leicester wins the game by 16 runs in one of the most stunning
turnarounds in First-Class cricket.

PM Chatterjee 10-20

If you haven't heard of George Geary, it is even less likely that you have come across the name of Premangshu Chatterjee.

Chatterjee was a left arm medium pace bowler who played for Bengal in India's Ranji Trophy in the 1940s and 50s. Despite his lack of genuine pace, he had the uncanny ability to swing the ball on any surface.

His contemporary Sujit Mukherjee, once described facing him: "*The ball was by no means new when I went in, but I found it curving and dipping as if with a life of its own. Premangshu bowled round the wicket and barely at medium pace, but was apparently able to swing the ball all day on any ground in Calcutta ... three times I looked for the ball everywhere, and three times my bat was nowhere near the ball as it swung in, pitched and whisked away ... The fourth ball was of fuller length, way outside the off-stump, and I put my left leg right across and prepared to push it firmly away into the covers. I am sure I went through all the motions correctly, but again missed the ball – which, this time, did not miss my leg-stump.*"

Chatterjee finished his First Class career having taken 134 wickets at 17.75 apiece. But his crowning glory came in a Ranji Trophy match against Assam played at Jorhat in 1957.

With a formidable batting line up led by one of India's greatest opening batsmen Pankaj Roy, Bengal bats through almost two full days of the four day match to score 505.

Premangshu Chatterjee then comes in to bowl his left armed medium pace, and immediately starts swinging the ball prodigiously.

In a remarkable 19-over spell, Chatterjee gets the opener Guha Roy caught in the slips with an outswinger he is unable to take the bat away from, and then runs through the rest of the side with in swinging deliveries that are virtually unplayable. The Assam innings folds up for a paltry 54, with Chatterjee taking all ten wickets giving away only 20 runs.

Assam follows on and makes 245, but Bengal wins the match by an innings and 206 runs.

Premangshu Chatterjee's 10-20 remains *the best bowling figures ever achieved in First Class cricket outside The United Kingdom*, and the third best figures of all time.

Albert Ernest Vogler 10-26
Bert Vogler was a South African leg break bowler who had a mean googly. Much to the dismay of contemporary batsmen, he also combined the speed of Anil Kumble and the flight and turn of Shane Warne in the same delivery. Just to confuse the batsmen further, he was also a good fast medium bowler who often opened the bowling.

In the first decade of the 20th century, he was reputed to be the most difficult bowler in the world to bat against and was named Wisden Cricketer of the year in 1908.

Vogler played 15 Tests for South Africa, taking 64 wickets at 22.73 apiece. His First Class figures were even more impressive with 393 wickets bought at just over 18 runs each. He was also an accomplished middle order batsman in both formats of the game.

Bert (or Ernie) Vogler, will however remain immortal for a Currie Cup match that was played in December 1906 between Eastern Provinces and Griqualand at Johannesburg.

Eastern Provinces scores a massive 403 with Bert Vogler contributing 79. Vogler opens the bowling with his fast medium, picks up two wickets and soon switches to leg breaks and takes four more. He ends up with figures of 6-12 and Griqualand is all out for 51.

Griqualand follows on and this time, Vogler changes his tactics. He opens the bowling, and in tactics that would be used by the likes of MS Dhoni a hundred years later, he starts with his leg breaks.

The effect is simply devastating.

Vogler runs through the Griqualand batting on his own this time. When the opposition is dismissed for a second time that day at the identical score of 51, Bert Vogler's figures read 12-2-26-10.

A hundred years on, this remains *the best bowling figures ever achieved in the game in the Southern Hemisphere.*

Albert Moss 10-28

Cricket was a bowler's game in the nineteenth century. A law change in 1884 outlawed any covering of the pitch once play was under way, which meant conditions could change drastically during a match, usually in the bowler's favour. A wet pitch that was drying out would produce uneven bounce and still have enough moisture for the ball to move off the seam.

Born in the English town of Coalville, Leicestershire, in 1863, Albert Moss was the second of six children to Edward and Ann Moss. He immigrated to New Zealand in 1889, a decision that would transform the record books.

It is December 1889 at Christchurch, and Canterbury is playing Wellington. Albert Moss has just come up the ranks thanks to his club performances and is making his debut for Canterbury in a First Class match.

Canterbury scores 138 on a difficult pitch and rain ends the day early. The next morning Wellington comes in to face Moss on a wicket that is tailor made for his style of fast bowling which depended on movement off the pitch.

Moss is in his elements and in a performance never before or after seen in New Zealand, he runs through the entire Wellington line up taking 10 wickets for 28 runs in his 19.3 overs. Wellington is dismissed for 71. Moss then takes 3 wickets in the second innings and Canterbury wins the match by 33 runs.

Despite the talent, Moss was to go on to play only 4 First-Class matches in total. He was tried and convicted for trying to murder his new wife with an axe, but on grounds of insanity, jailed for five years then deported to Rio de Janeiro. There he was to recover his mental strength, join the Army and have a successful career.

He was also to marry his childhood English sweetheart and wife for a second time when Mary moved to Rio after she learnt he had recovered.

But Albert Moss was never to play cricket again.

This article was originally published in 'The Roar' on January 27, 2017.

Have fat, can bat: Cricketers who were worth their weight in gold

"The ground was getting a bit too far away."

– WG Grace, explaining his decision to retire at the age of 50

Images: WG Grace and Warwick Armstrong

Fitness and a lean body are clearly grossly overrated, for there have been many cricketers through the ages who have not believed in this adage and gone on to have careers, some long and some a trifle shorter, at the highest level.

So why give up on good food when you are so good that fitness doesn't matter?

Sir WG Grace would never have passed muster as a sprinter, but mid-way through his career, the good Doctor could have faced up to a Sumo wrestler with some degree of confidence. And yet that didn't seem to affect his cricket.

54,000 First Class runs and 2800 wickets at an average below 18, don't suggest that his girth was ever a concern to him. Except at the fag end of his Test career, when at the age of 50 he retired from Test Cricket saying rather regretfully, "*The ground was getting a bit too far away.*"

Warwick "The Big Ship" Armstrong was estimated to weigh around 21 stone (133kg) when he captained Australia after the First World War – but it didn't seem to affect him much, as he won his first eight Tests in charge, all against England, including the first Ashes whitewash, in 1920-21.

He scored six Test hundreds, a triple-century in First Class Cricket, and for good measure took 87 wickets with his leg spin.

Edmund Blunden described it best in Cricket Country: "*He made a bat look like a teaspoon, and the bowling weak tea; he turned it about idly, jovially, musingly. Still he had but to wield a bat – a little wristwork – and the field chased after the ball in vain. It was almost too easy.*"

He didn't particularly like being heckled about his weight though.

Jack Fingleton recounted an episode from a Sheffield Shield match when Armstrong retrieved a ball from the fine-leg boundary: "*The big fellow ambled out after it, recovered the ball and was raising his arm to return the ball when a spectator at his back shouted: 'Come on Armstrong! Throw it in!' Armstrong at once dropped his arm, walked slowly back to his position in the slips, then softly lobbed the ball back to the bowler."*

Arjuna Ranatunga, the former captain of Sri Lanka is an immediate recall when we speak of generously endowed cricketers.

There is the famous story of the time when Shane Warne was trying to figure out how to get Ranatunga to step out so he could get him stumped. Wicket keeper Ian Healy who was always ready with a piece of advice, deadpanned: *"Put a Mars bar on a good length, that should do it."* Ranatunga, whose bat once sported an advert for 'Sam's Chicken and Ribs', shot back *"if you do, I bet David Boon will get there first."*

Ranatunga, remarkably, was also a part-time bowler, who occasionally unleashed his military medium-pace. In a One-Day International (ODI) against India at Kanpur in 1986, the hosts were chasing only 196 to win. Ranatunga produced astonishing figures of 6-1-14-4 and bundled India out for 78.

But he couldn't, or didn't, run, between the wickets or on the field, even if his life depended on it. He would call for runners and substitutes pretty regularly and irk opposing captains. But all of that fades away when you remember the late cut he played off Glenn McGrath to hand Sri Lanka their only World Cup trophy to date.

No account of cricket's big men can ever exclude the outrageously talented Inzamam-ul-Haq.

It seemed the link between the big man's brain and his legs had major breakdowns when he batted. Surprisingly, the link worked fine when he was playing his delectable strokes.

At the start of his career, his running between the wickets was a series of laughs - a big guy calling for a run, calling it off, and then calling again and getting stranded midway with a totally bewildered look on his face. It could not possibly have got worse from there!

And indeed it improved, because he got smarter. He hit more boundaries, ran ones when others would have run threes, and most times, he just turned his back on his partner! If he hadn't been a brilliant batsman and a genuinely gentle giant, he probably wouldn't have lasted as long as he did.

An average of 50 from 120 Test matches with 25 centuries, after all, has to be some recompense for a few missed runs.

This article was originally published in 'The Roar' on October 22, 2016.

The summer of '48 and two of the greatest wicketkeepers of all time

"What are the main essentials of wicket-keeping? Really, There are two - an ability to sight the ball early and then to catch it, whether it comes from a delivery, a hit, or a throw-in." – Alan Knott

Images: Don Tallon and Godfrey Evans

The Summer of 1948 was a truly unique one.

After the ravages of six years of war and continuing rationing, the stoic English men, women and children welcomed the Australian team with open arms when they crossed the seas for the first Ashes tour since the end of the Second World War.

While a strong Australian team and the prospect of Ashes cricket for the first time in nearly a decade captured the public's imagination, for the leader of the team, Donald Bradman, who was on his farewell tour, they reserved their unabashed adulation.

People all over England and Scotland braved the vagaries of weather and turned up in their thousands for every one of the 34 fixtures on that tour. And for the 23 in which The Don put in his appearance, the crowds queued up from the previous night, waiting through rain and mist, sitting in the open for hours, waiting for the time when Bradman would bat.

Every time he came out to bat, and every time he went back to the pavilion, the applause and the love for the genius of the man was amply evident.

The love for Bradman was not entirely shared by the English cricket team, and understandably so.

He was a man on a mission in his last series as an Australian captain and player, and determined to come back home without a loss from the almost six-month long series. He was not about to give any quarter and stumble at the last hurdle as his predecessors had done in 1902 and 1921, losing in the final festival match.

Bradman took every one of the 34 matches in that 1948 series seriously, making sure his team did not let up, even when he himself was not playing. And when he played, he ensured the opposition were ground to dust.

The approach didn't win him many friends, either in the opposition or within his own team.

One of Bradman's closest friends was Walter Robins, one of the English selectors. Allegations flew thick and fast that Bradman had a hand in selecting the English Test teams to ensure the strongest team did not take the field. Unfounded perhaps, but they would not go away, as the Australians piled up success after success.

Keith Miller, for one, fancied himself as a batsman. But Bradman knew Miller and Lindwall, with their blistering speed and ability to bowl bouncers to Englishmen not used to that kind of pace and bounce, in a series where the ball was replaced every 55 overs, were a far more potent weapon than wasting Miller as a batsman in a team loaded with excellent wielders of the willow.

Being mates with the likes of Bill Edrich and Godfrey Evans from his wartime services in England, and at the best of times a less than taciturn man, Miller made no secret of his discontent, especially when the bowling overload caused his series batting average to be lower than Lindwall's, a man not known for his batting.

Sidney Barnes, for another, firmly believed himself to be a better batsman than Bradman and was determined to outscore him during the series. The fact he failed in this was never far from his mind.

Notwithstanding these internal and external battles on and off the field, and the debate about how strong the English cricket team was in 1948 after losing a generation of fast bowlers unable to develop in their prime years due to the war, Don Bradman's team won the Ashes.

They also came away as the first and undoubtedly the last undefeated side to complete such a tour of the British Isles, and irrevocably and for all time to come, earned themselves the sobriquet of '*The Invincibles*'.

But while all this was taking place on and off the field that summer of 1948, an almost unnoticed rivalry was on display between two of the greatest wicketkeepers the world has ever seen.

Don Tallon and Godfrey Evans were separated by team rivalry but joined by their genius behind the stumps.

Don Tallon

If there was one thing that Bradman and his 1948 teammate and mercurial all-rounder Miller agreed on, it was that Don Tallon was the best wicketkeeper ever.

Miller's opening partner, and the fastest bowler of his time, Lindwall, agreed. The Don even included him as wicketkeeper in his all-time XI – a team that stretched across time from Clarrie Grimmett to Sachin Tendulkar.

Writing in *Cricket Country*, Arunabha Sengupta aptly described Tallon thus: "*Unusually tall for a stumper, Tallon crouched nearly double as the bowler started out on his run-up and remained motionless until he had seen all that he needed to know from the delivery – pace, flight, spin and swerve. His keeping was characterised by neat and unhurried work, alert and agile, especially superlative on the leg side. Ground was covered with easy movements, catches were made with perfect technique and little fuss, stumpings were carried out with subtle, surgical precision. Indeed, his 131 stumpings in First-Class cricket hardly saw the removal of anything but a dignifiedly flicked single bail.*"

Debuting against an English side for a Queensland Country XI at Toowoomba in 1932-33 when he was sixteen, Tallon's first victim was Herbert Sutcliffe.

Bradman was a fan and wanted him in the 1938 Ashes side but was outvoted at the selection committee meeting and Victoria's Ben Barnett was chosen instead to sail for England.

Tallon had missed his chance.

By the time the Second World War broke out, Tallon had equalled E Pooley's long-standing world record of twelve victims in a match (it has yet to be beaten) for Queensland against New South Wales in Sydney during the 1938-39 season. He had six victims in each innings, catching nine of them and stumping three.

His prime years were, however, to be spent on the battlefields, away from the 22 yards.

Tallon joined the Australian Army in 1940 and was discharged three years later, afflicted with painful stomach ulcers. A successful surgery thereafter took away a part of his stomach but allowed him to get back to the game he loved.

When cricket resumed after the war, Tallon was a clear leader in the race for the wicketkeeping spot in the Australian team, with Bert Oldfield now retired, Barnett's four years as a prisoner of war of Japan in Singapore leaving him in no condition to play, and Charlie Walker having been killed by Nazi pilots over Soltau in Germany.

He finally made his Test debut against New Zealand at Wellington in 1946, but it would be a couple of years before he would know it.

It was only in 1948 that the match was given Test status. His first dismissal was an *"exceptionally smart piece of stumping"* off Bill 'Tiger' O'Reilly, the great leg-spinner appearing his final Test.

And so on to 1948 and the Invincibles tour.

Wisden said in his obituary a few decades later *"Having made the wicket-keeping place his own against England in 1946-47, and established what was then a record twenty victims in the series, he was an integral part of Bradman's brilliant 1948 side in England, being equally at home whether keeping to the speed of Lindwall and Miller or the spin of Johnson, McCool and Ring."*

But that doesn't even begin to tell us about Tallon the man or the 'keeper.

Quite appropriately, if trifle insensitively, known by his nickname 'Deafy', Tallon was a very quiet man, probably due to a lifelong medical condition that affected his hearing. He got his nickname in a county game on that tour when, unusually, he was the only Australian not to appeal for a snicked catch. Ron Hamence said, "What's the matter with you these days? You must be deaf as well as dumb."

The name stuck.

His teammate, Doug Ring, said, *"All he used to do was grin at you. He hardly said anything to you. He'd gamble: he and Keith Miller used to have bets on who'd hit the next four and that sort of thing. He played cards and he smoked incessantly, of course, but he rarely said anything at all."*

But on the field, under Bradman's captaincy, Tallon turned into such a vociferous appealer that the English complained that he was intimidating the umpires.

He was also the butt of practical jokes but took it all rather well.

Colin McCool, who had a frustrating series as he rarely got a game due to Bradman exploiting the 55 over rule to the hilt by primarily bowling his pace bowlers, took his entertainment where he could. He was fascinated by the wicketkeeper's habit of never unpacking.

"He was the only man I ever met who literally lived out of a case on tour. He rarely unpacked when we arrived at a new hotel, and if he wanted a clean shirt he simply rummaged about in his case until he found one, then stuffed the dirty one back in."

During one of their county games, McCool discovered a hatch in the wardrobe connecting their room to Miller and Lindwall's. Tallon, as usual, dumped his bags on the floor. The fast bowlers came in and goaded him into unpacking.

McCool describes what followed: *"Slowly he shook out his dress suit, placed it on a hanger, walked over to the wardrobe and hung it on the rail. While we all talked loudly and cheerfully, Lindwall nipped down the corridor into his own room and grabbed the suit through the hatch. Again Tallon advanced on the wardrobe, again he hung up a suit. It was when he went there for the third time that he twigged something was wrong ... There's never been such an expression as there was on 'Deafy''s face when he peered into that wardrobe and realised that the suits he had hung there half a minute before had all disappeared. Miller and Lindwall were in such a state I thought we might be without a fast attack for the Test match."*

But on the field, Tallon was having a fabulous tour and showing the world what they had missed out on during the war years. He was blossoming fully in the narrow window of opportunity that life had given him.

Tallon's 21 Tests brought him 50 catches and eight stumpings. During the Invincibles tour, the Australian team strategy of primarily depending on pace bowling saw Tallon make 12 catches and no stumpings during the Tests.

However, Bradman rested his lead pace bowlers, Miller and Lindwall, during the tour games to save energy for the Tests and allowed the spinners do more work so that, overall, Tallon took 29 catches and 14 stumpings for the tour. A stunning record.

A couple of remarkable catches on that tour did no harm in building Tallon's legend.

In the second Test at Lord's, Washbrook inside edged a Toshack full toss directly downwards at Tallon's ankle. Bradman described the catch as "*miraculous*" because Tallon had to reach so low, so quickly, in order to take the catch.

Neil Harvey's account was more detailed as he was substituting for Lindwall at cover-point: "*Tallon was standing up to the wicket. Toshack bowled a full toss, which was very foreign for him. Washbrook couldn't believe his luck. He shaped up to whack it past me. He went back, got an edge, and Tallon caught it on the full at his boot-tops. I've never seen a catch like it. He was a freak behind the stumps. From Toshack's hand to Tallon's gloves, no pitch was involved. Fantastic catch!*"

The Tallon legend was forever sealed in the final Test at the Oval, when England had a horrible outing, getting all out for 52. The score would have been far less but for a dour, dogged 30 in 130 minutes with one four from Len Hutton. And the only reason Australia was able to dismiss Hutton was because of Tallon.

Lindwall bowled an inswinger that Hutton leg-glanced. He might, Bradman said, "*reasonably have looked for a boundary. Instead, he saw Tallon move across with uncanny anticipation, scoop the ball in his outstretched left glove as it sped towards earth, turning a somersault but serenely holding the ball aloft. No greater catch has been seen behind the wickets.*"

Tallon missed the 1949-50 series against South Africa due to stomach ulcers and a bout of unemployment, but was selected for all the Tests at home against England. He had a decent series, and while few could dispute his supremacy with the gloves, Tallon was fast losing his hearing. This was to cut short his career further.

He went to England with the 1953 side, but was a pale shadow of his former self. He played the first Test at Trent Bridge, but was then replaced by Gil Langley for the rest of the Tests and never played for Australia again.

His opposite number Godfrey Evans described him as the "*best and most nimble keeper ever*". His teammate and all-rounder, Alan Davidson, paid him the ultimate compliment, calling him the "*Bradman of 'keepers*".

Godfrey Evans

Godfrey Evans held 816 catches and carried out 250 stumpings in his first-class career – a total of 1,066 dismissals, all this from 465 matches, including 219 in Tests (173 catches and 46 stumpings).

He was also a reliable batsman, with 14,882 runs (average 21.22), including 2,439 in Tests (average 20.49), and two centuries.

At the crease, he was perhaps best known for his stand against Australia in Adelaide in 1947, when he batted for a record 97 minutes without a run as he stoically helped his partner, Denis Compton, score a century and save the match.

What made Evans' reputation as a 'keeper stand out even more is the fact that he was playing for Kent, which produced both Les Ames and Alan Knott, and despite that, Evans was widely acknowledged to be the best of the three.

David Foot, writing for the *Guardian*, put it very eloquently: "*Many keepers cloak their skills in anonymity, judged by an efficiency that is missed by the naked eye. Not Evans. He possessed an innate theatricality, never too irritating or counter-productive, evident in the marvellous way he hurled himself for those legside catches with those red gloves that seemed slightly too big for him. He was perpetually bobbing around on his toes, bracing himself to chase in front of the stumps in search of a run-out; or standing up, intrepid and reliable, to wily medium-paced bowlers. He was so nimble, so intuitive, that a great many of his legside dismissals were more like optical illusions.*"

Evans was a perfectionist and hated letting byes through. Writing an obituary on the death of his friend, Frank Keating was to say: "*In a rain-ruined match on a difficult Oval pitch [1946], India scored 331 in their only innings – and Godfrey let through a solitary bye. He would remember it to his dying day 53 years later: 'Do you know, I still wake up sometimes cursing myself for that wretched, idiotic little bye. Jim Langridge, twirly left-arm, Sussex, remember him? He floated down this silly little blighter outside off stump; it might have kept a bit low, but I took my eye off it for a fraction and it scuttled through. I didn't half swear at myself. Still do.'*"

Making his debut in England's first post-war series against India in 1946, Evans was in fine form and richer by a significant amount of experience by the time the Invincibles came to town.

The magic of Godfrey Evans was visible from the very start of the series.

In the first Test at Nottingham, with Bradman walking in to bat on an English Test ground for the first time in a decade, Barnes, who was on 62 and looking for his century, went back to Laker and under-edged a cut. It struck Evans's thigh and looped over the keeper's head in the direction of fine leg.

Malcolm Knox, writing in *Bradman's War*, provides four eyewitness versions of what occurred in the next two seconds:

Bradman: "*Evans' catching of Barnes [was] one of the most miraculous feats of recovery as well as acrobatics one would see in a long time.*"

Jack Fingleton: "*Evans dived back like a rugby winger going for the line in an international …*"

Bill O'Reilly: "*… a corkscrew backward dive, sizing up to Olympic Games standards.*"

Godfrey Evans: "*I just saw this little blob in the sun and dived towards it instinctively and caught it one-handed.*'

Knox says, "*So astounding was Evans's effort, umpire Cooke couldn't decide if it was a catch. He referred it to Chester, who gave it out. Barnes said to Evans: 'I didn't believe you had caught me –I didn't think you COULD have caught that ball.*"

As was exemplified by Keating's words on him, Godfrey Evans hated making mistakes, whether it was letting a bye through or dropping a catch.

One of his enduring frustrations was that he never caught or stumped Bradman while keeping to more than 1400 runs off his bat in Australia and England.

When the Test series was over, and the Australians were playing Kent at Canterbury and Bradman was in his fifties, he chopped down on a ball from Eddie Crush. Evans stifled an appeal.

Later, Bradman said, laughing, "*You are a fool, Godfrey; you've been trying to get me all these years and you threw away the perfect chance out there.*"

"*Did you hit it then, Don?*"

"Of course I did ... I hit it hard. There was your chance, and when you got it, Godfrey, you didn't take it."

The regret was to live on to the end of his days, for that was the last first-class match he would play against Bradman.

Evans did not particularly like Bradman's ruthlessness, but as a man, he was big-hearted, and the war had taught him the value of looking at things with a larger lens than one's own narrow perspective.

When Eric Hollies bowled Bradman for nought in The Don's last innings, among all the chest beating and remonstrations, from behind the stumps his take was philosophical: *"What is a nought in such a fabulous career, even such a nought at such a time?"*

Evans played on for another decade until his last match against India in 1959 and was one of the mainstays of an English team which rose from the post-war ashes to once again decisively capture the cricketing crown from an Australia sans Bradman in the 1950s.

In later life, Evans was the resident expert for the bookmakers Ladbrokes, reassessing the odds at each twist and turn of a Test, usually getting it right, but, at Headingley in 1981 when he offered England at 500 to one, he famously got it wrong thanks to Bob Willis' 8 for 43. Ladbrokes, we understand, forgave him for that one overenthusiastic call.

A more exuberant wicketkeeper and human being has not been seen on the cricket field, before or since. David Frith perhaps described him best, when he called Evans *"biologically incapable of being downhearted."*

The England bowler Mike Selvey, now a *Guardian* cricket correspondent, played with him when Evans was 56 years old in a fun seven-a-side game at The Oval.

"*My experience was an education. Late out-swing just whispered into his gloves. I slipped in a full-length in-swinger on leg stump – the most difficult to take – and there he was, down the leg side as if by telepathy, flicking the bails away as the batsmen changed feet.*"

Selvey said he had never seen a better display of wicket-keeping.

Don Tallon and Godfrey Evans: two gloved geniuses with vastly different personalities who shared centre stage and reached the peaks of their prowess behind the stumps during a magical summer of post-war cricket that would forever remain a part of cricketing lore.

This article was originally published in 'The Roar' on May 18, 2017

When West Indies met their Waterloo in Ireland

"Where were you when the West Indies were skittled at the Holm Field?"

— A common question still asked at Holm Field, Sion Mills, Ireland

Image: Holm Ground at Sion Mills, Ireland

Almost to the day, 154-years after Emperor Napoleon's dreams of conquering the world were shattered on the once beautiful fields of Waterloo, Garry Sobers' West Indian cricket team faced their own little Waterloo in the picturesque ground of Sion Mills in Ireland.

No one outside Londonderry in Northern Ireland had ever heard of Sion Mills before that day, but the astonishing events that took place in July 1969 ensured the cricketing world would remember the name for ever more.

Waterloo cost Napoleon and the Duke of Wellington and their allies a combined 65,000 men in casualties and losses.

While the loss of life on the fields of Sion Mills was not as heavy (in fact everyone survived to tell the tale), the grievous harm done to the reputation and combined egos of the mighty West Indians was no less devastating.

West Indies were in the process of rebuilding into what would later become a team to rival Don Bradman's 1948 Invincibles.

But at this stage, it was still work in progress and they had just lost the Test series 2-0 to England, with their last match at Lord's ending in a thrilling draw, a match the visitors could on another day, have won.

As soon as the Test was over, the team, minus Garry Sobers and Lance Gibbs who were injured, had left for Ireland.

Arunabha Sengupta recounted in his version of the match in *Cricket Country*: "*Having ended the second Test, the team had made a dash from St John's Wood to Heathrow to catch a late flight to Belfast. The drive to the Inter Counties Hotel in Lifford had been long. The restaurant at the hotel had already closed by the time they arrived after midnight. The team ate at a nearby late night restaurant and stretched out their tired bodies in their hotel rooms. The only drinking that had taken place that evening had involved the Irish.*"

The sunny morning of the match brought little cheer to the weary West Indians when they got to the ground and realised that the overnight rains had left the ground and the pitch in less than ideal conditions for cricket.

Depending on whose account you chose to follow, the pitch was either diabolical or merely required a bit of application to bat on.

In his account Sengupta says: "*On walking in, both the openers inserted a finger in the pitch. Both their fingers went in all the way. Batting was going to be a nightmare.*"

Derek Scott, writing his account in Cricket Europe Ireland, says: "*The wicket was not bad but due to rain it was damp and had a good deal of grass. The ball came through at varying heights but it was slow. The West Indies had come from fast conditions and played some fast wicket shots which got them out.*"

They two accounts could well be talking of different matches given how divergent they are in their reproach of the pitch.

Without getting into a debate on the exact state of that pitch that July day in 1969, let's just say the wicket was less than ideal, when Basil Butcher, captaining the side in place of the injured Sobers, agreed to bat, so that the nice crowd that had gathered with pints of Guinness in their hands, could enjoy watching the visitors make some runs in the swashbuckling style one had always heard about.

Dougie Goodwin and Alec O'Riordan opened the bowling for Ireland. Facing them were the two West Indian openers, Joey Carew and Steve Camacho.

Camacho faced up to O'Riordan and took one run off the first over.

West Indies, 1 for no loss.

In attempting to hook Goodwin's first ball however, Camacho was caught at midwicket in the next over. In O'Riordan's second over Carew also attempted an equally ill-conceived hook, the ball got up too high and he lobbed a catch to square leg.

West Indies 1 for 2.

Maurice Foster came in at the fall of Carew's wicket and was foolishly run out as Basil Butcher hit a ball to Patrick "Podge" Hughes' left at mid-off and called a run. Hughes fielded the ball and his throw to the wicket-keeper easily beat Foster who was not hurrying.

West Indies 3 for 3.

This brought in Clive Lloyd.

Butcher and Lloyd got three singles. In 0'Riordan's sixth over, one ball reared up and struck Butcher on the arm. He angrily slashed at the next and Gerry Duffy, one of Ireland's great Cricketers, took a good low catch at gully.

West Indies 6 for 4.

43-year-old manager of the West Indies team, Clyde Walcott, who had retired 10-years previously, had agreed to play the match for the sake of the spectators. He now came in, after exchanging some angry words with the departing batsmen, who he felt (perhaps justifiably so), had thrown away their wickets.

The out of practice but sensible and experienced Walcott stayed on the back foot as was proper on this wicket. In Goodwin's seventh over Clive Lloyd mis-drove a ball to mid-off where Robin Waters, Ireland's opening batsman, took an easy catch.

West Indies 6 for 5.

In Goodwin's next over, John Shepherd played a bad cut shot at a short ball and Duffy took another good catch at gully to make the West Indies 8 for 6.

Walcott and Mike Findlay (who was later to himself become the Manager of the West Indies team) were together for six overs; when the score was 12 Walcott had made all six runs scored since he had come in.

Not too bad for a retiree!

In Goodwin's 11th over Findlay stepped out to drive and spooned the ball to mid-off where Waters almost fumbled the easy catch.

West Indies 12 for 8.

Ireland conceded a bye and then O'Riordan took two wickets with the last two balls of his 12th over. Walcott swung at him and John Anderson caught a skier at cover. Next ball Pascall Roberts swung to leg and skied to the wicket-keeper.

Goodwin then bowled a maiden over to Philbert Blair, the fast bowler, but O'Riordan in his last over conceded 12 runs to Grayson Shillingford and Blair with both swinging their bats. This effectively more than doubled the score. With the fifth ball of the next over Goodwin bowled Blair and it was all over.

West Indies all out for 25.

It was a stunning turn of events that had the crowd on their feet and cheering their two boys. The entire innings had lasted 86 minutes.

O'Riordan had astonishing final figures of 13-8-18-4 and Goodwin 12.5-8-6-5.

Ireland opened their batting 25-minutes before lunch and quickly hit up a 125 runs for the loss of eight wickets before declaring and leaving West Indies 95-minutes to bat again.

Either the wicket had dried sufficiently for the West Indians to be able to bat normally again, or the ignominy of having scored the lowest total of any team (in any form of cricket) against Ireland, was playing on their minds.

West Indies scored 78 for 4 in their second innings before the teams called it a day, leaving Ireland the winners by virtue of their first innings lead.

Captain Butcher led from the front, scoring a chance less half century. But as Sengupta recounts, the team was not about to forgive Butcher for his decision to bat first on that pitch: "*Maurice Foster called Butcher a submarine captain because he preferred to bat under water. Carew disagreed, saying Butcher was not fit to captain a submarine.*"

A match that has gone down in West Indian cricketing history as a match they would rather forget.

The last word on the West Indian performance, aptly enough, came from LD Roberts, a correspondent of Jamaica's Gleaner, who, seeing the West Indian flag flying upside down at the ground, remarked, "*Half-mast might have been more appropriate.*"

This article was originally published in 'The Roar' on March 24, 2017

A tale of two debuts: The Banerjee-Warne story

I'm proud of what I've achieved in cricket, as once I didn't think I was good enough.– Shane Warne

Image: Shane Warne

It was one of those exceptional Test matches that did not throw up a victor, but was never short on drama.

The year is 1992 and on a warm January morning, on the only pitch in Australia that has a reputation as a turner, India and Australia clash at the SCG for the third Test match of the series.

And they seem to have vastly different perspectives on the pitch.

In deference to the pitch's reputation, notwithstanding the hard surface and the sunny skies, Australia favours wrist spin and replaces off-spinner Peter Taylor with debutant leggie Shane Warne.

Meanwhile, India replaces slow left-arm spinner Venkatapathy Raju with a fourth fast bowler, debutant Subroto Banerjee. On that first day, under the blue skies, and on the hard pitch, India's decision looks the better one.

With Kapil Dev and Manoj Prabhakar unable to get a breakthrough, Indian captain Mohammad Azharuddin hands the ball to the Banerjee ahead of Javagal Srinath.

Banerjee is immediately effective.

In a debut spell that any fast bowler would be proud of, he first dismisses opener Geoff Marsh, knocking back his stumps. Mark Taylor and David Boon then have almost a century run partnership as Banerjee is taken off by Azhar. As soon as he is brought back in, Banerjee dismisses Taylor, getting him to edge a ball leaving him to wicketkeeper Chandrakant Pandit. Then he gets Mark Waugh to offer a catch to Prabhakar on 5.

In a wonderful 18-over spell, giving away only 47 runs, the unassuming boy from Bihar has dismissed three of the top batsmen in the world.

Boon remains not out on 129 and Australia is finally dismissed the next day for 313, thanks to Boon's knock.

The Indian batsmen then play magnificently, with Ravi Shastri scoring a superb double century, and a young Sachin Tendulkar remains not out on a mature 148, becoming the youngest man to score a Test century in Australia.

The weather plays truant with bad light and rain, causing 94.1 overs to be lost on the third and fourth days.

A tired Ravi Shastri is finally dismissed for 206 runs when Dean Jones takes a catch to give the Australian debutant Shane Warne his first Test wicket.

Unlike his fellow debutant, Warne's figures are not so impressive. He bowls 45 overs and picks up that sole wicket, conceding 150 runs.

India bats on until the fifth morning, before being finally dismissed for 483, taking a 170-run lead. While many believe the tourists have left it too late, Kapil, Prabhakar and Srinath pick up a wicket each, and then Shastri gets into the act on a pitch which is turning and now uneven, picking up four wickets for 45 runs.

Border and Warne manage to bat out the remaining overs to finish at 8-173, just eight runs ahead of India.

Bizarrely, the man who has bowled so well in the first innings, Subroto Banerjee, does not get to bowl a single ball in the second innings.

In fact, he never gets to bowl another ball in Test cricket, and is destined to be forever referred to in cricketing history as a one-Test wonder.

The other debutant, who takes one wicket for 150 runs, retires from Test cricket 15 years later as arguably the greatest spin bowler in the history of the game, having taken an astonishing 708 wickets in 145 Test matches.

As Rob Steen was to write in an article in Cricinfo earlier this year, *"First impressions are always a precarious matter, and never more so than in Sydney in 1992. Given that, of the two debutants, one dismissed Mark Taylor, Mark Waugh and Geoff Marsh cheaply while the other wound up with 1 for 150, one might be forgiven for suspecting that Subroto Banerjee would be the name now celebrated globally. Yet Banerjee never played another Test, while Warne symbolises the embrace of risk that underpins the very best sport has to offer."*

Banerjee ends the tour at the top of the averages with 15 runs per wicket. Javagal Srinath, his fellow pacer, finishes at the bottom, with 55 runs per wicket.

An Australian fan on *The Roar* tells me many years later, *"I was there that day at the SCG when Subroto Banerjee was bowling. And he was so impressive, I remember saying to my mates that India have found another fast bowler in the mould of Kapil Dev. I am still astounded that Banerjee never played another Test for India."*

Was it a case of just being unlucky, or as was often the case in India until recently, was it the lack of a 'godfather' in the system and the unfortunate victimisation by the zonal selection quota system in play? We shall never know.

Banerjee eventually decided to give up the fruitless quest to get back into the Indian Test side and after a few years moved to Australia, marrying a local girl. There he qualified to become a coach, to finally have the second innings spell he was denied so many years ago at the SCG.

And that second innings is proving of immense value to both countries.

For a six-month period, Banerjee was a coach to Mitchell Starc, who is currently shattering the stumps of triple centurions in India. He was also instrumental in shaping up the bowling action and style of India's top fast bowler, Umesh Yadav, who calls Banerjee his mentor.

Yadav, after that stint with Banerjee, has been an unrecognisable bowler over the past year or so.

With the word now out on the street that Banerjee has for some time been giving pointers to a certain Arjun Tendulkar to prepare him for the higher level of the game, besides enjoying his successful assignment as coach of the Jharkhand team, Banerjee's second innings may well turn out to be even more valuable than his first.

Cricket will surely be the richer for it.

This article was originally published in 'The Roar' on March 11, 2017

Head and shoulders above the rest

"Lady, if I were built in proportion I'd be eight foot ten!" –
Joel Garner

Images: Glenn McGrath and Mitchell Starc

Vivian Richards. Sachin Tendulkar. Sunil Gavaskar. Brian Lara.

None of them make the cut. They just didn't have it in them.

Virat Kohli. Steven Smith. Kane Williamson.

They don't make it either. The bar, unfortunately, is set too high for these wonderful cricketers.

In fact, the bar is set several inches higher than the longest hair on the highest pate on that list - at 6 feet 5 inches to be precise.

As the discerning reader has guessed by now, I am indeed talking about the search for the tallest cricketers to have ever played to form a team that would (literally) have to stoop to conquer. Mind you, this is no easy task, for, not surprisingly, most of the tallest cricketers to have played the game were bowlers. And fast bowlers at that.

The height from which the ball comes at incredible speed, the bounce it generates and the angles it achieves, not to mention the sheer intimidation factor, are stuff that the worst pre-dawn nightmares of batsmen are made of.

But it would be a mistake to assume that the tall men only make it to the highest levels of cricket as bowlers. On the contrary, a journey through the ages brings up accounts of enough vertically advantaged players to create a real conundrum about who to pick for our playing XI.

Prudence demands, however, that given how injuries are a regular feature of modern-day cricket, we pick a squad of 14 to ensure that players have ample time to recover while they are on tour, playing the top teams in the world comprised of players not so well-endowed as themselves in the height department.

So then, as Maria says in The Sound of Music, let's start at the very beginning.

Opening the batting for our GOC (Giants of Cricket) XI are two players with sharply contrasting approaches to batting. At the top of the order is Will Jefferson, at 6'10", the tallest opener to have ever played professional cricket. Jefferson was an attacking batsman with a range of strokes, and made his debut for Essex in 2000. He played 119 first-class matches, averaging just below 36, with a high score of 222 and 17 centuries to his credit. An injury-plagued career meant, however, that Jefferson retired in 2012, never having played for England.

The perfect foil to Jefferson is Michael Vandort from Sri Lanka. At 6'5", Vandort just about makes the cut in this team. And that is more than can be said about the rather unfortunate international career of this talented left-hander from Colombo. For years, Vandort waited for a chance to open the batting for Sri Lanka. But a set combination of Sanath Jayasuriya and Marvan Atapattu denied him. He played against Bangladesh in 2002 when the seniors were rested, scored a century and then waited three and a half years before he played again. In all, Vandort played 20 Tests, scoring 1144 runs at an average of 37 with four centuries. And now, at the age of 37, opening the batting for the GOC XI is perhaps the most he can expect out of the rest of his career.

At No. 3 in comes "Two-Metre Peter" Fulton, at 6'6", the tallest New Zealand batsman to have ever played the game at this level. Fulton came into the limelight with a free-flowing 301 not out for Canterbury against Auckland in 2003. Although he had an intimidating presence when he was at the crease, and in form, in a career spanning 23 Tests he could only average 25 with two centuries. But in a team of big men, on his day, Fulton - who would also be a back-up opener, given he often did the job for New Zealand too - is a menacing presence at the top of the order.

Occupying the No. 4 slot (where he should have played instead of being sacrificed as an opening batsman), is Tom Moody. At 6'7", Moody was capable of hitting through the covers and along the ground with great power. He was a very good slip fielder, in the best tradition of Australian top-order batsmen, and a natural leader of men to boot. He was also a useful medium-pace swing bowler. While his record is at best reasonable in his eight Tests, he played 76 ODIs for Australia with some success and was a member of two World-Cup winning squads.

At No. 5, a position he played the most at for England through the 1970s, is the captain of the GOC XI and the most complete cricketer in the world of his time: Tony Greig, 6'6". Greig dominated the cricket field, with confidence and charisma to match his height. With 3599 Test runs, eight centuries and a batting average over 40 to go with a haul of 141 wickets in 58 Test matches, Greig was a true all-rounder.

Greig is followed at No. 6 by left-hand batsman and right-arm fast-medium bowler Jacob Oram. At 6'6" New Zealand's Oram walks into this team as a dominating modern-day all-rounder. A hard-hitting batsman and a useful fast-medium bowler, Oram suffered successive injuries that cut short his career. He was a far better all-rounder than his batting average of 36 and bowling average of 33 in 33 Tests suggests.

At No. 7 is the absolute oxymoron in cricket: a tall wicketkeeper. At 6'5", Adrian Rollins was an opening batsman by choice but a wicketkeeper by default. Derbyshire asked him to keep in 1993, and Rollins did the job admirably, considering the average wicketkeeper is usually a foot shorter. For the GOC XI, Rollins is the hands-down favourite for the job.

The embarrassment of riches that the fast-bowling department offers us from a height perspective must be well used, for it's the bowling that is the cornerstone of any formidable cricket team. Opening the bowling at 6'7" is a man who terrified the best batsmen in the world for 12 years between 1988 and 2000. Curtly Ambrose's specialty was in utilising the "corridor of uncertainty", and in extracting uneven bounce on any surface in the world. No one who has followed cricket in the last few decades will ever forget Ambrose's spell in Perth in 1993, when, as the vaunted Australian batting lay in tatters, Ambrose's spell on the scoreboard showed an incredible 7 wickets for 1 run in 32 deliveries.

Ambrose's opening ball partner will ensure that the already demoralised batsmen have no time to recover. At 6'5", given the mastery and accuracy of his fast bowling, the height factor was almost irrelevant for Australia's Glenn McGrath. The (almost) undisputed greatest Australian fast bowler of all time was one of the most difficult bowlers in the world to face, as his 563 Test wickets at 21.64 and 381 ODI wickets at 22.02 will testify.

Replacing Ambrose after his fiery opening spell is an inclusion that may surprise some: Mitchell Starc of Australia. At 6'6", with fast deliveries swinging into the right hander and Wasim Akram-like yorkers, Starc can often be unplayable. At the 2015 World Cup, his 22 victims at 10.18 runs per wicket earned him the Player-of-the-Tournament award, and an automatic place in our GOC XI.

To round things off, at a towering 6'8" is "Big Bird" Joel Garner, a mainstay of the fearsome West Indian pace attack of the 1980s, with his toe-crushing yorkers and unplayable bouncers. With 259 Test wickets at an average below 21, Garner was an awesome sight to behold. When he ran in with those loping strides, your stumps often lay shattered before you could say "Big Bird".

With these 11 unbelievable cricketers at our disposal, the GOC XI looks like a line-up that every team in the world needs to be afraid of. And as back-up, making up the squad of 14, are three players who are clearly unlucky to be left out of the playing XI for the first match.

It is only fitting that the 12th man is someone who is still young and fit: the current West Indies captain, measuring in at 6'7", Jason Holder, an all-rounder with a lot of promise and plenty of guts and determination.

As a back-up to Starc, we have one of his predecessors from the Australian national side, Bruce Reid. A similar left-arm fast bowler,

Reid at 6'8" is the tallest Australian to play Test cricket till date. He was a big part of the Australian attack in the late-1980s but injuries caused him to retire early.

To complete the 14, we have the tallest cricketer to ever play at the highest level. At 7'1", Mohammad Irfan of Pakistan. The incredible bounce that he gets from a great height and the natural angle of the left-arm fast bowler make him a difficult customer to handle.

With that, the GOC XI is all set to go on the road. Any takers?

This article was originally published in 'ESPN Cricinfo' on January 16, 2017

Meltdown at the death: It is just not cricket

"If the sound of an ice-cream truck was the soundtrack to your cricketing youth, then the sound of silence is the backdrop to a collapse."

— *Brendon Julian*

Image: Jana Novotna after the 1993 Wimbledon Final

March 23rd 2016, **Bangalore**: Two runs to get in the last three balls of the WT20 and the chance to knock India out of the World Cup at home.

Unheralded part time bowler Hardik Pandya bowls the last over with the Bangladeshi middle order still at the crease.

The result - In their eagerness to win the game quickly, two batsmen hole out in the deep, Pandya bowls the last ball wide off the crease, and MS Dhoni sprints up to the wicket and runs out Mustafizur Rahman who has set off for a desperate game tying run.

And we have the mother of all meltdowns. India lives to fight another day with the Aussies, who they would defeat to go through to the semis.

February 8th 2016, Hamilton: It is Brendon McCullum's swansong ODI. He has a good game and scores a swashbuckling 47, but the Kiwis spectacularly collapse, losing five wickets for nine runs chasing 246 against Australia, and getting bowled out in the 46th over.

January 20th 2016, Canberra: Chasing 349 to win, India is 277 for 1 with Shikhar Dhawan scoring 126 and Virat Kohli 106, and then it happens. India loses the last nine wickets for 46 runs and the last three wickets in 11 balls for the addition of one run.

India loses the match and suffers the ignominy of going down 4-0 in the five-match ODI series. A meltdown to remember.

June 17th 2014, Mirpur: Chasing 106 to win in an ODI against India, and at 44 for 2, Bangladesh spectacularly collapses for 58 all out, creating several records.

They lose eight wickets for 14 runs, the third lowest runs scored for an eight-wicket collapse in ODIs. They allow India to achieve the lowest score successfully defended by a team after being bowled out. They allow a part time bowler, Stuart Binny, to achieve bowling figures of six wickets for four runs, the best ever bowling performance by an Indian in ODI.

Clearly, a meltdown of stupendous proportions.

These are hardly the only instances of teams collapsing and snatching the proverbial defeat from the jaws of victory. The history of cricket abounds with such stories. Without trying to single out India as the worst culprit, but just looking at them as an example, several instances come to mind.

Losing nine wickets for 49 runs and being all out for 88 chasing 288 against the Kiwis in 2000. Losing eight wickets for 29 runs and being all out for 91 runs chasing 249 against the Proteas in 2006. And of course the most infamous of them all, losing seven wickets for 22 runs to lose the World Cup semis against Sri Lanka at Calcutta in 1996, the match that effectively launched Sri Lanka as a top tier cricketing nation.

So what is it about these meltdowns?

How can top teams with players in form and with an enormous reservoir of experience, collapse spectacularly under pressure? Is it just the pressure cooker like situation, is it a lack of application, experience, presence of mind? Or maybe these are just isolated examples in a cricketing world which by and far follows the script of 'may the better team win'.

Either way, it's worth thinking about and seeking parallels from the world of sports outside cricket.

April 10th 2011, Augusta: A 21-year old golfing genius called Rory McIlroy enters the final round of the Augusta Masters leading by four strokes, a big margin by any standards. On the first five holes, he misses three easy putts, but still turns for home in the lead.

On the 10th hole however, it all falls apart. Starting with the tee off where he hooks a drive (the ball curved left as he hit it) and it lands on a hill between two cabins where a golf ball had never been seen to land before, it rapidly goes south, with Rory taking seven strokes to do a Par 4. He eventually makes a hash of the next three holes to finish 10 strokes behind the winner, South African Charl Schwartzel.

Sports lexicon has something called the '*Steve Blass Disease*' – a term which is used now for all kinds of sports choking. Steve Blass, who played baseball for the Pittsburgh Pirates, was one of the most feared pitchers in major league baseball.

He made his debut in 1964 and terrified batters for the next eight years. But then over a course of a few weeks he completely lost his ability to throw (and he had no physical problem), but before every game, he was petrified.

This lasted for the rest of his shortened career.

But Blass was hardly the only one. There was Jimmy White, the snooker player. He lost six snooker world championship finals and in 1994 muffled a simple black put which would have given him victory against Stephen Hendry.

Wimbledon 1993 saw Jana Novotna, up 4-1 in the final set against Steffi Graf, double faulting her way to defeat and weeping on the shoulders of The Duchess of Kent.

So what is it about choking or about meltdowns? Clearly, it happens across individual and team sports, across nationalities and situations, and from the Golf greens of Augusta to the green top of Eden Gardens.

It cannot all be explained by match fixing or drugs or betting or incompetence. After all these are sportsmen at the peak of their physical prowess, in most cases, representing their country with pride.

The answer appears to be a simple fact, that we are finally human beings.

Research suggests that choking affects most of us at one time or the other – it can be at a job interview, on a date, in an exam, and most often, when we are on public display.

When we walk, we don't think about how we move our body. But when we walk up on stage to receive a certificate or an award, we are acutely conscious of every step. And what puts the pressure is the negativity associated with failure.

If you win a match for your country, you are a hero. If you choke, and lose, you lack courage and are a failure.

So when it comes to the crunch, and victory is in sight, you want to get it quickly. And in trying to do so you lose two wickets, and then you lose two more, and before long you are so panicked that you have a spectacular team collapse like any of the above.

Or you lead 4-1 in a Wimbledon final, and in your anxiety to finish the match you start trying harder, and double fault your way to a loss, giving up your only chance to be a champion.

So choking is human.

These are young men and women. Yes, they are young men and women who get paid well, but like all human beings, they can fail at crucial moments, and they do.

This doesn't make them lesser human beings, and this certainly doesn't make them cheaters and match fixers. Let's lay off them, take the media and social pressure off, and let them come back to entertain us again.

This article was originally published in 'The Roar' on March 31, 2016

The Invincibles on my wall: The story of the 1948 Australian team sheet

"Bradman's 1948 Australians in a performance so brilliant and so full of character as to compel respect from the losers, and admiration from even their most devoted supporters." – John Arlott

Image: The 1948 Invincibles 'Team Sheet'

The many coloured inks of the 18 signatures on the Australian 'team sheet' have long dried. The signatories have all passed on but for the youngest member of the side.

But the stories around those 56 days on the voyage and the 112 days of brilliant cricket (of the 144 days spent on tour in Great Britain), have become the stuff of lore, taking on a life of their own in the telling and re-telling over the past 69 years.

It has often been asked, was the 1948 Australian side the best Test team of all time?

Were they better than Clive Lloyd's West Indies of the 1980s which boasted the jaw-dropping exploits of Vivian Richards that were all but overshadowed by the most fearsome battery of fast bowlers cricket has ever known?

Were they better than Steve Waugh and Ricky Ponting's Australia of the Nineties and Noughties, who beat all comers?

Were they better than Warwick Armstrong's 1921 side which hammered the English on that tour when nothing that the home team did could stop the juggernaut?

Those are debates that will go on forever, and there will never be a clear answer, and indeed there should not. For greatness does not need to be counted in the singular.

What is not open to debate is that on the 1948 tour of Great Britain, the Australians under Donald Bradman played 31 first-class fixtures and three other games across the length and breadth of England and Scotland, and did not lose a single match. They thus became the first

Test team to tour Britain and not lose a match, earning themselves the sobriquet of 'The Invincibles'.

In the Summer of '48, Don Bradman, at the age of 40, led a team of players across the oceans with intent, with resolve, with enormous talent in their ranks, and with the dogged will to win all that they could.

They showed the world that, at least for that wonderful post-war summer, they were truly Invincible.

After years of destruction and loss of human life, and in a Britain where the populace continued to face rationing, this Australian team brought back the joy of cricket at its very best. Bradman had announced before the tour that it was going to be his last and, combined with the Australians' swashbuckling style on the field and the swagger on and off it, this was a breath of fresh air to the thousands clamouring to get into the grounds to witness history being made.

While the result of the tour was not uniformly pleasing to the peoples of the two nations, the quality of the cricket was of the highest order.

The 1948 Australian team, besides Bradman, comprised Lindsay Hassett (vice-captain), Arthur Morris (co-opted selector), Sid Barnes, Bill Brown, Ron Hamence, Neil Harvey, Ian Johnson, Bill Johnston, Ray Lindwall, Sam Loxton, Colin McCool, Keith Miller, Doug Ring, Ron Saggers, Don Tallon, and Ernie Toshack.

Other than the 26 of the 31 first-class matches, they won four of the five Tests (drawing the third at Manchester thanks to rain) by, successively, eight wickets, 409 runs, seven wickets, and an innings and 149 runs. Bradman and his batsmen failed to make 200 only twice on the entire tour, while his bowlers dismissed the opposition for less than 200 an astonishing 37 times, and seven times for under 100. They scored more than 350 twenty-four times, while the highest score against them outside the Tests was 299 by Nottinghamshire.

Bradman's men won half their 34 matches by an innings. The team's 50 centuries were shared by 11 players, seven of whom passed 1000 runs.

Those are staggering numbers, for any team, under any circumstances. When it is achieved on a single tour over a three month period, it is truly astounding. It is little surprise the team earned the Invincibles tag.

It is also no surprise therefore that something like the side's official team sheet, which is a single sheet of paper autographed by this incredible team, should be a treasured item.

Frank Keating, writing in *Cricinfo* almost 20 years ago, described how as a ten-year-old in 1948, he sent off his autograph book to Don Bradman with a request to sign and mail it back to him:
"I posted my autograph book off to Worcester, with an SAE for safe return. It contained a few Gloucestershire heroes from the summer before, and I addressed it to Mr Donald Bradman himself. By return came a single sheet. The whole touring party had signed. What awestruck privileged joy."

I can fully appreciate how he felt, for I felt that joy and thrill in no small measure when I received my own copy a few weeks ago in the post, even if mine was not despatched to me by The Don himself.

Keating wrote:

"Half-a-century on, I see them still, headed by the captain's neatly rhythmic joined-together writing: 'D. G. Bradman'- both full-stops meticulously in place. I drooled over the neat upright 'W. A. Brown' and the cack-handed, more squiggly 'A. R. Morris' and his fellow leftie apprentice, schoolboyish 'Neil Harvey'.

School-masterly and precisely formed was 'R. A. Hamence', but 'Colin McCool' and 'D Ring' were almost illegible hieroglyphics, as you might expect from leg-spin tweakers.

And the mesmerising all-rounder hero stood out, of course, seeming to sign 'eith iller' in a readable sub-copperplate, and then adding the capitals K and M in a couple of gorgeously bold and flowery flourishes.

The two wicket-keepers' hands were both trim, straight-forward and standing up: 'Don Tallon' and 'R. A. Saggers'."

All is not as it seems however, as far as this particular set of autograph sheets is concerned.

If one looks a bit closer, the mercurial Sidney Barnes' signature does not quite appear next to his name, nor exactly on the ruled line it is supposed to be confined to, and seems almost printed on the paper.

And, as always with Barnes, there is a story behind it.

As Keating explained, and contemporary accounts testify, *"on the liner Strathaird coming over, captain Bradman and manager Keith Johnson, both hot on PR, had given each player a huge sheaf of these blank sheets headed by the Australian crest and told them to sign each one and then pass them on. In all, 5000 were filled. It was a fearful chore, and only the ferret-sharp Barnes had been ready for it. Before embarking he had made a rubber stamp bearing his signature, and when his turn came, he apparently paid a pocket-money pittance to a youthful shipmate to stamp his 5000."*

What is delightful about this little shenanigan, is that, while none of the 5000 'team sheets', including the ones owned by Frank Keating and myself, have Barnes' actual signature, its mere absence and substitution by a rubber stamp, cleverly inserted, in some strange way, makes these sheets even more unique.

Poetic as Keating's eloquence is however, what I see on that parchment is a bit different from what he observed.

Where he saw Bradman's *"neatly rhythmic joined-together writing"*, I see the bold stroke of the pen that is still solidly imprinted on the page, put there by that same supremely firm right hand which guided the bottom of the bat as the ball sped to all parts of the ground while The Don accumulated his 50,371 runs.

On that last tour, Bradman scored 2428 runs in the 23 first-class matches that he played, at an average just below 90, with 11 centuries, leaving plenty of memories for his fans to cherish.

Where he saw the great Keith Miller, *"adding the capitals K and M in a couple of gorgeously bold and flowery flourishes"*, I see the image of my favourite dashing war hero running in, gripping the red cherry firmly in his right hand as he prepares to hand out some 'chin music' to the next, hapless batsman.

Miller, with his barrage of short-pitched bowling, helped subdue Len Hutton and Dennis Compton, England's best batsmen, and took the wind out of the English sails. He made life so difficult for Hutton, that England dropped him for the third Test. In all first-class matches on the tour, Miller took 56 wickets at 17.58 and scored 1088 runs at an average of 47.30.

After Bradman, the firmest hand on that page is of the man who opened the bowling with Miller, a bowler I would have given anything to be able to see perform at his peak. His Ashes opponent, John Warr, held that "*if one were granted one last wish in cricket, it would be the sight of Ray Lindwall opening the bowling in a Test match*".

In that 1948 series, Lindwall took 27 wickets in Tests, 86 on the tour. Jack Robertson, a Middlesex opener good enough to play for England, ended in hospital with a broken jaw. Compton was carried off, in the middle of a courageous 145 at Old Trafford, after trying to hook a no ball.

A cricket writer in England said of Lindwall, "*Most of his cricket was played at the highest level, on the best wickets and against strong opposition. His skill, unaccompanied by histrionics, was something for the connoisseur to savour.*"

And then there is Keating's "schoolboyish" signatory, Neil Harvey. At 19 years of age, Harvey was the youngest member of the touring party, and at the time, the youngest Australian to have scored a Test century, when he made 153 against India during the previous Australian summer.

Speaking about Harvey's selection, Bradman had uttered these prophetic words, *"He has the brilliance and daring of youth, and the likelihood of rapid improvement."*

I wonder, as the youngest member of the squad, and his junior by some 13 years, was Harvey the "youthful shipmate" that Keating refers to, who was made to apply the "Sidney Barnes" rubber stamp 5000 times during that 28-day voyage? If that was indeed the case, it is a bizarre twist in the tale.

Harvey had to wait until the fourth of the five-Test series before he could get into the Test XI, and making place for him was an injured Barnes!

Harvey scored 112 in a first innings counter-attack to keep Australia in contention after they had suffered a top-order collapse. Harvey then hit the winning boundary in the second innings, as Australia took the match with a Test world record successful run-chase of 3-404.

He retained his place for the fifth Test, ending the series with 133 runs at a batting average of 66.50.

The members of that 1948 team, but for Neil Harvey, have all passed on, as sadly has the brilliant Frank Keating. The tales of The Invincible tour will, however, continue to be told long after the current keepers of the few surviving team sheets, including myself, are gone.

And coming generations of cricket fans will continue to react with awe at the achievements of that group of brilliant cricketers who brought back the simple joy of enjoying cricket to a world torn apart by war.

In the meantime, for the coming decades, my personal piece of Invincibles history will adorn my study wall, telling me stories of that magnificent summer of 1948.

This article was originally published in 'The Roar' on April 19, 2017

The Last Word

The history of cricket is a fascinating one.

For a game, that in its present form, is less than 150-years old at the highest level, it has managed to acquire an eclectic collection of quirky characters, tremendous drama on an ongoing basis, great performances that keep getting better through the ages and some once in a lifetime performers like Don Bradman, who is counted among the greatest sportsmen the world has ever seen.

The game has evolved through various experiments and phases and we are in the happy situation that there are three formats of the game at the highest level, all of which have their followers.

The purists will have nothing but Test Cricket, the '*instant gratification*' group will have nothing but the T20, and the many in between will refuse to give up on the strategic importance of the middle 20-overs of the ODI format, vehemently opposing a shorter version of the ODI.

And cricket is thus far happy to cater to all three while it fills up the archives with stories that people like me bring to life for future generations to reflect on and learn from.

I hope you enjoyed reading the collection of thought pieces as much as I enjoyed writing them. Thank you for joining my growing readership among cricket lovers across the world.

Cover photo: Smiling Study of Donald Bradman by Sam Hood (1872-1953), is from the collection of the State Library of New South Wales.[hood_05518]

Please follow my writing and recommended reads on

www.cricketwriter.com

I can also be followed on Twitter **@Cric_Writer**

See you in the Autumn of 2017 with ***Spell-binding Spells***.

Appendix – The Scorecards

Australia in England 1896 (2nd Test)

Venue	Old Trafford, Manchester on 16th, 17th, 18th July 1896 (3-day match)
Balls per over	5
Toss	Australia won the toss and decided to bat
Result	Australia won by 3 wickets
Umpires	A Chester, J Phillips

Close of play day 1 Australia (1) 366/8 (Kelly 14*, McKibbin 7*)

Close of play day 2 England (2) 109/4 (Ranjitsinhji 41*)

Australia first innings		Runs	Balls	Mins	4s	6s
FA Iredale	b Briggs	108		220	16	-
J Darling	c Lilley b Richardson	27		35		-
G Giffen	c and b Richardson	80		110		-
*GHS Trott	c +Brown b Lilley	53				
SE Gregory	c Stoddart b Briggs	25				
H Donnan	b Richardson	12				
C Hill	c Jackson b Richardson	9				
H Trumble	b Richardson	24				
+JJ Kelly	c Lilley b Richardson	27				
TR McKibbin	not out	28				
E Jones	b Richardson	4				
Extras	(6 b, 8 lb, 1 w)	15				
Total	(all out, 170 overs)	412				

Fall of wickets:

1-41 (Darling), 2-172 (Giffen), 3-242 (Iredale), 4-294 (Trott), 5-294 (Gregory), 6-314 (Donnan), 7-325 (Hill), 8-352 (Trumble), 9-403 (Kelly), 10-412 (Jones, 170 ov)

England bowling	Overs	Mdns	Runs	Wkts	Wides	No-Balls
Richardson	68	23	168	7	1	-
Briggs	40	18	99	2	-	-
Jackson	16	6	34	0	-	-
Hearne	28	11	53	0	-	-
Grace	7	3	11	0	-	-
Stoddart	6	2	9	0	-	-
Lilley	5	1	23	1	-	-

England first innings		Runs	Balls	Mins	4s	6s
AE Stoddart	st Kelly b Trott	15				
*WG Grace	st Kelly b Trott	2				
KS Ranjitsinhji	c Trott b McKibbin	62				
R Abel	c Trumble b McKibbin	26				
FS Jackson	run out	18				
JT Brown	c Kelly b Trumble	22				
AC MacLaren	c Trumble b McKibbin	0				
+AFA Lilley	not out	65				
J Briggs	b Trumble	0				
JT Hearne	c Trumble b Giffen	18				
T Richardson	run out	2				
Extras	(1 b)	1				
Total	(all out, 90 overs)	231				

Fall of wickets:

1-2 (Grace), 2-23 (Stoddart), 3-104 (Abel), 4-111 (Ranjitsinhji), 5-140 (Jackson), 6-140 (MacLaren), 7-154 (Brown), 8-166 (Briggs), 9-219 (Hearne), 10-231 (Richardson, 90 ov)

Australia bowling	Overs	Mdns	Runs	Wkts	Wides	No-Balls
Jones	5	2	11	0	-	-
Trott	10	0	46	2	-	-
Giffen	19	3	48	1	-	-
Trumble	37	14	80	2	-	-
McKibbin	19	8	45	3	-	-

England second innings (following on)		Runs	Balls	Mins	4s	6s
AE Stoddart	b McKibbin	41				
*WG Grace	c Trott b Jones	11				
KS Ranjitsinhji	not out	154		185	23	-
R Abel	c McKibbin b Giffen	13				
FS Jackson	c McKibbin b Giffen	1				
JT Brown	c Iredale b Jones	19				
AC MacLaren	c Jones b Trumble	15				
+AFA Lilley	c Trott b Giffen	19				
J Briggs	st Kelly b McKibbin	16				
JT Hearne	c Kelly b McKibbin	9				
T Richardson	c Jones b Trumble	1				
Extras	(2 b, 3 lb, 1 w)	6				
Total	(all out, 90.1 overs)	305				

117

Fall of wickets:

1-33 (Grace), 2-76 (Stoddart), 3-97 (Abel), 4-109 (Jackson), 5-132 (Brown), 6-179 (MacLaren), 7-232 (Lilley), 8-268 (Briggs), 9-304 (Hearne), 10-305 (Richardson, 90.1 ov)

Australia bowling	Overs	Mdns	Runs	Wkts	Wides	No-Balls
Jones	17	0	78	2	-	-
Trumble	29.1	12	78	2	-	-
McKibbin	21	4	61	3	1	-
Giffen	16	1	65	3	-	-
Trott	7	1	17	0	-	-

Australia second innings		Runs	Balls	Mins	4s	6s
FA Iredale	b Richardson	11				
J Darling	c Lilley b Richardson	16				
G Giffen	c Ranjitsinhji b Richardson	6				
*GHS Trott	c Lilley b Richardson	2				
SE Gregory	c Ranjitsinhji b Briggs	33				
H Donnan	c Jackson b Richardson	15				
C Hill	c Lilley b Richardson	14				
H Trumble	not out	17				
+JJ Kelly	not out	8				
TR McKibbin	did not bat					
E Jones	did not bat					
Extras	(3 lb)	3				
Total	(7 wickets, 84.3 overs)	125				

Fall of wickets:

1-20 (Iredale), 2-26 (Giffen), 3-28 (Trott), 4-45 (Darling), 5-79 (Gregory), 6-95 (Donnan), 7-100 (Hill)

England bowling	Overs	Mdns	Runs	Wkts	Wides	No-Balls
Richardson	42.3	16	76	6	-	-
Briggs	18	8	24	1	-	-
Hearne	24	13	22	0	-	-

Scorecard Courtesy www.cricketarchive.com

Australia in British Isles 1948 (4th Test)

Venue	Headingley, Leeds on 22nd, 23rd, 24th, 26th, 27th July 1948 (5-day match)
Balls per over	6
Toss	England won the toss and decided to bat
Result	Australia won by 7 wickets
Umpires	HG Baldwin, F Chester

Close of play day 1 England (1) 268/2 (Edrich 41*, Bedser 0*)
Close of play day 2 Australia (1) 63/1 (Hassett 13*, Bradman 31*)
Close of play day 3 Australia (1) 457/9 (Lindwall 76*, Toshack 12*)
Close of play day 4 England (2) 362/8 (Evans 47*, Laker 14*)

England first innings		Runs	Balls	Mins	4s	6s
L Hutton	b Lindwall	81		187		-
C Washbrook	c Lindwall b Johnston	143		317	22	-
WJ Edrich	c Morris b Johnson	111		314	13	1
AV Bedser	c and b Johnson	79		177	8	2
DCS Compton	c Saggers b Lindwall	23		55		-
JF Crapp	b Toshack	5				
*NWD Yardley	b Miller	25				
K Cranston	b Loxton	10				
+TG Evans	c Hassett b Loxton	3				
JC Laker	c Saggers b Loxton	4				
R Pollard	not out	0				
Extras	(2 b, 8 lb, 1 nb, 1 w)	12				
Total	(all out, 192.1 overs)	496				

Fall of wickets:

1-168 (Hutton), 2-268 (Washbrook), 3-423 (Bedser), 4-426 (Edrich), 5-447 (Crapp), 6-473 (Compton), 7-486 (Cranston), 8-490 (Evans), 9-496 (Laker), 10-496 (Yardley, 192.1 ov)

Australia bowling	Overs	Mdns	Runs	Wkts	Wides	No-Balls
Lindwall	38	10	79	2	-	-
Miller	17.1	2	43	1	-	-
Johnston	38	12	86	1	1	1
Toshack	35	6	112	1	-	-
Loxton	26	4	55	3	-	-
Johnson	33	9	89	2	-	-
Morris	5	0	20	0	-	-

Australia first innings		Runs	Balls	Mins	4s	6s
AR Morris	c Cranston b Bedser	6				
AL Hassett	c Crapp b Pollard	13				
*DG Bradman	b Pollard	33	56	59		-
KR Miller	c Edrich b Yardley	58				2
RN Harvey	b Laker	112		188	17	-
SJE Loxton	b Yardley	93		135	8	5
IWG Johnson	c Cranston b Laker	10				
RR Lindwall	c Crapp b Bedser	77				
+RA Saggers	st Evans b Laker	5				
WA Johnston	c Edrich b Bedser	13				
ERH Toshack	not out	12				
Extras	(9 b, 14 lb, 3 nb)	26				
Total	(all out, 136.2 overs)	458				

Fall of wickets:

1-13 (Morris), 2-65 (Hassett), 3-68 (Bradman), 4-189 (Miller), 5-294 (Harvey), 6-329 (Johnson), 7-344 (Loxton), 8-355 (Saggers), 9-403 (Johnston), 10-458 (Lindwall, 136.2 ov)

England bowling	Overs	Mdns	Runs	Wkts	Wides	No-Balls
Bedser	31.2	4	92	3	-	2
Pollard	38	6	104	2	-	1
Cranston	14	1	51	0	-	-
Edrich	3	0	19	0	-	-
Laker	30	8	113	3	-	-
Yardley	17	6	38	2	-	-
Compton	3	0	15	0	-	-

England second innings		Runs	Balls	Mins	4s	6s
L Hutton	c Bradman b Johnson	57				1
C Washbrook	c Harvey b Johnston	65				1
WJ Edrich	lbw b Lindwall	54				1
DCS Compton	c Miller b Johnston	66				
JF Crapp	b Lindwall	18				
*NWD Yardley	c Harvey b Johnston	7				
K Cranston	c Saggers b Johnston	0	2		-	-
+TG Evans	not out	47				
AV Bedser	c Hassett b Miller	17			4	-
JC Laker	not out	15				

R Pollard	did not bat	
Extras	(4 b, 12 lb, 3 nb)	19
Total	(8 wickets, declared, 107 overs)	365

Fall of wickets:

1-129 (Washbrook), 2-129 (Hutton), 3-232 (Edrich), 4-260 (Crapp), 5-277 (Yardley), 6-278 (Cranston), 7-293 (Compton), 8-330 (Bedser)

Australia bowling	Overs	Mdns	Runs	Wkts	Wides	No-Balls
Lindwall	26	6	84	2	-	-
Miller	21	5	53	1	-	-
Johnston	29	5	95	4	-	3
Loxton	10	2	29	0	-	-
Johnson	21	2	85	1	-	-

Australia second innings		Runs	Balls	Mins	4s
AR Morris	c Pollard b Yardley	182		291	33
AL Hassett	c and b Compton	17		74	1
*DG Bradman	not out	173	292	255	29
KR Miller	lbw b Cranston	12		30	2
RN Harvey	not out	4			1 -
SJE Loxton	did not bat				
IWG Johnson	did not bat				
RR Lindwall	did not bat				
+RA Saggers	did not bat				
WA Johnston	did not bat				
ERH Toshack	did not bat				
Extras	(6 b, 9 lb, 1 nb)	16			
Total	(3 wickets, 114.1 overs)	404			

Fall of wickets:

1-57 (Hassett), 2-358 (Morris), 3-396 (Miller)

England bowling	Overs	Mdns	Runs	Wkts	Wides	No-Balls
Bedser	21	2	56	0	-	1
Pollard	22	6	55	0	-	-
Laker	32	11	93	0	-	-
Compton	15	3	82	1	-	-
Hutton	4	1	30	0	-	-
Yardley	13	1	44	1	-	-
Cranston	7.1	0	28	1	-	-

Scorecard Courtesy www.cricketarchive.com

England in South Africa and Zimbabwe 1999/00 (5th Test)

Venue	Centurion Park, Centurion on 14th, 15th, 16th, 17th, 18th January 2000 (5-day match)
Balls per over	6
Toss	England won the toss and decided to field
Result	England won by 2 wickets
Umpires	DB Hair, RE Koertzen
TV umpire	CJ Mitchley
Referee	BN Jarman
Close of play day 1	South Africa (1) 155/6 (Klusener 22*, Pollock 9*; 45 overs)
Close of play day 2	No play
Close of play day 3	No play
Close of play day 4	No play
Man of the Match	MP Vaughan

South Africa first innings		Runs	Balls	Mins	4s	6s
G Kirsten	c Adams b Gough	0	7	4	-	-
HH Gibbs	c Adams b Caddick	3	21	35	-	-
JH Kallis	b Caddick	25	61	81	2	1
DJ Cullinan	c and b Mullally	46	91	153	5	-
*WJ Cronje	c Maddy b Gough	0	6	8	-	-
PC Strydom	c Stewart b Silverwood	30	41	61	5	-
L Klusener	not out	61	96	171	7	1
SM Pollock	run out (Hussain)	30	64	70	3	-
+MV Boucher	b Mullally	22	48	60	4	-
PR Adams	not out	4	8	5	1	-
M Hayward	did not bat					
Extras	(2 b, 11 lb, 11 nb, 3 w)	27				
Total	(8 wickets, declared, 329 minutes, 72 overs)	248				

Fall of wickets:

1-1 (Kirsten, 0.6 ov), 2-15 (Gibbs, 7.6 ov), 3-50 (Kallis, 18.1 ov), 4-55 (Cronje, 19.6 ov), 5-102 (Strydom, 33.1 ov), 6-136 (Cullinan, 40.3 ov), 7-196 (Pollock, 56.6 ov), 8-243 (Boucher, 70.3 ov)

123

England bowling

England bowling	Overs	Mdns	Runs	Wkts	Wides	No-Balls
Gough	20	2	92	2	1	10
Caddick	19	7	47	2	-	-
Mullally	24	10	42	2	1	1
Silverwood	7	1	45	1	1	-
Vaughan	2	0	9	0	-	-

England first innings

England first innings		Runs	Balls	Mins	4s	6s
MA Butcher	did not bat					
MA Atherton	did not bat					
*N Hussain	did not bat					
MP Vaughan	did not bat					
+AJ Stewart	did not bat					
CJ Adams	did not bat					
DL Maddy	did not bat					
AD Mullally	did not bat					
AR Caddick	did not bat					
D Gough	did not bat					
CEW Silverwood	did not bat					
Extras		0				
Total	(no wicket, declared, 0 minutes)	0				

South Africa second innings

South Africa second innings		Runs	Balls	Mins	4s	6s
G Kirsten	did not bat					
HH Gibbs	did not bat					
JH Kallis	did not bat					
DJ Cullinan	did not bat					
*WJ Cronje	did not bat					
PC Strydom	did not bat					
L Klusener	did not bat					
SM Pollock	did not bat					
+MV Boucher	did not bat					
M Hayward	did not bat					
PR Adams	did not bat					
Innings						

Forfeited

England second innings		Runs	Balls	Mins	4s	6s
MA Butcher	lbw b Klusener	36	84	110	6	-
MA Atherton	c Boucher b Pollock	7	29	41	1	-
*N Hussain	c Gibbs b Pollock	25	69	94	2	-
+AJ Stewart	c Boucher b Hayward	73	140	179	10	1
CJ Adams	c Boucher b Hayward	1	10	21	-	-
MP Vaughan	b Hayward	69	108	153	9	-
DL Maddy	run out (Kirsten->Boucher)	3	6	14	-	-
AR Caddick	c Boucher b Pollock	0	2	2	-	-
D Gough	not out	6	3	14	1	-
CEW Silverwood	not out	7	7	8	1	-
AD Mullally	did not bat					
Extras	(4 b, 9 lb, 7 nb, 4 w)	24				
Total	(8 wickets, 323 minutes, 75.1 overs)	251				

Fall of wickets:

1-28 (Atherton, 10.1 ov), 2-67 (Butcher, 25.5 ov), 3-90 (Hussain, 32.1 ov), 4-102 (Adams, 37.1 ov), 5-228 (Stewart, 69.3 ov), 6-236 (Maddy, 72.2 ov), 7-236 (Caddick, 72.4 ov), 8-240 (Vaughan, 73.5 ov)

South Africa bowling	Overs	Mdns	Runs	Wkts	Wides	No-Balls
Pollock	20	7	53	3	-	3
Hayward	17.1	3	61	3	3	3
Klusener	14	4	38	1	-	1
Kallis	13	2	44	0	1	-
Cronje	5	3	15	0	-	-
Strydom	6	0	27	0	-	-

Scorecard Courtesy www.cricketarchive.com

England in Australia 1936/37 (3rd Test)

Venue	Melbourne Cricket Ground, Melbourne on 1st, 2nd, 4th, 5th, 6th, 7th January 1937 (timeless match)
Balls per over	8
Toss	Australia won the toss and decided to bat
Result	Australia won by 365 runs
Umpires	GE Borwick, JD Scott
Close of play day 1	Australia (1) 181/6 (McCabe 63*, Oldfield 21*)
Close of play day 2	Australia (2) 3/1 (Fleetwood-Smith 0*, Ward 1*)
Close of play day 3	Australia (2) 194/5 (Fingleton 39*, Bradman 56*)
Close of play day 4	Australia (2) 500/6 (Bradman 248*, McCabe 14*)
Close of play day 5	England (2) 236/6 (Leyland 69*, Robins 27*)

Australia first innings		Runs	Balls	Mins	4s	6s
JHW Fingleton	c Sims b Robins	38	117	119	4	-
WA Brown	c Ames b Voce	1	17	29	-	-
*DG Bradman	c Robins b Verity	13	21	28	-	-
KE Rigg	c Verity b Allen	16	51	45	1	-
SJ McCabe	c Worthington b Voce	63	146	144	6	-
LS Darling	c Allen b Verity	20	54	56	1	-
MW Sievers	st Ames b Robins	1	23	22	-	-
+WAS Oldfield	not out	27	65	81	3	-
WJ O'Reilly	c Sims b Hammond	4	19	19	-	-
FA Ward	st Ames b Hammond	7	13	10	-	-
LO Fleetwood-Smith	did not bat					
Extras	(2 b, 6 lb, 2 nb)	10				
Total	(9 wickets, declared, 65.3 overs)	200				

Fall of wickets:

1-7 (Brown), 2-33 (Bradman), 3-69 (Rigg), 4-79 (Fingleton), 5-122 (Darling), 6-130 (Sievers), 7-183 (McCabe), 8-190 (O'Reilly), 9-200 (Ward)

England bowling	Overs	Mdns	Runs	Wkts	Wides	No-Balls
Voce	18	3	49	2	-	-

Allen	12	2	35	1	-	-
Sims	9	1	35	0	-	-
Verity	14	4	24	2	-	-
Robins	7	0	31	2	-	-
Hammond	5.3	0	16	2	-	-

England first innings		Runs	Balls	Mins	4s	6s
TS Worthington	c Bradman b McCabe	0	4	2	-	-
CJ Barnett	c Darling b Sievers	11	34	27	2	-
WR Hammond	c Darling b Sievers	32	88	81	4	-
M Leyland	c Darling b O'Reilly	17	49	41	1	-
JM Sims	c Brown b Sievers	3	15	27	-	-
+LEG Ames	b Sievers	3	23	19	-	-
RWV Robins	c O'Reilly b Sievers	0	2	1	-	-
J Hardstaff	b O'Reilly	3	3	6	-	-
*GOB Allen	not out	0	2	9	-	-
H Verity	c Brown b O'Reilly	0	3	1	-	-
W Voce	not out	0	4	3	-	-
Extras	(5 b, 1 lb, 1 nb)	7				
Total	(9 wickets, declared, 28.2 overs)	76				

Fall of wickets:

1-0 (Worthington), 2-14 (Barnett), 3-56 (Leyland), 4-68 (Hammond), 5-71 (Sims), 6-71 (Robins), 7-76 (Ames), 8-76 (Hardstaff), 9-76 (Verity)

Australia bowling	Overs	Mdns	Runs	Wkts	Wides	No-Balls
McCabe	2	1	7	1	-	-
Sievers	11.2	5	21	5	-	-
O'Reilly	12	5	28	3	-	-
Fleetwood-Smith	3	1	13	0	-	-

Australia second innings		Runs	Balls	Mins	4s	6s
WJ O'Reilly	c and b Voce	0	1	1	-	-
LO Fleetwood-Smith	c Verity b Voce	0	7	13	-	-
FA Ward	c Hardstaff b Verity	18	75	68	-	-
KE Rigg	lbw b Sims	47	120	122	3	-
WA Brown	c Barnett b Voce	20	39	43	1	-
JHW Fingleton	c Ames b Sims	136	428	386	6	-
*DG Bradman	c Allen b Verity	270	375	458	22	-

		Runs	Balls	Mins	4s	6s
SJ McCabe	lbw b Allen	22	51	43	2	-
LS Darling	b Allen	0	1	1	-	-
MW Sievers	not out	25	86	71	1	-
+WAS Oldfield	lbw b Verity	7	28	23	1	-
Extras	(6 b, 2 lb, 10 nb, 1 w)	19				
Total	(all out, 149.7 overs)	564				

Fall of wickets:

1-0 (O'Reilly), 2-3 (Fleetwood-Smith), 3-38 (Ward), 4-74 (Brown), 5-97 (Rigg), 6-443 (Fingleton), 7-511 (McCabe), 8-511 (Darling), 9-549 (Bradman), 10-564 (Oldfield)

England bowling	Overs	Mdns	Runs	Wkts	Wides	No-Balls
Voce	29	2	120	3	-	-
Hammond	22	3	89	0	-	-
Allen	23	2	84	2	-	-
Verity	37.7	9	79	3	-	-
Robins	11	2	46	0	-	-
Sims	23	1	109	2	-	-
Worthington	4	0	18	0	-	-

England second innings		Runs	Balls	Mins	4s	6s
TS Worthington	c Sievers b Ward	16	95	82	1	-
CJ Barnett	lbw b O'Reilly	23	57	45	4	-
WR Hammond	b Sievers	51	92	78	7	-
M Leyland	not out	111	212	194	11	-
+LEG Ames	b Fleetwood-Smith	19	44	34	3	-
J Hardstaff	c Ward b Fleetwood-Smith	17	22	16	2	-
*GOB Allen	c Sievers b Fleetwood-Smith	11	11	8	1	-
RWV Robins	b O'Reilly	61	68	65	7	-
H Verity	c McCabe b O'Reilly	11	25	15	1	-
JM Sims	lbw b Fleetwood-Smith	0	3	2	-	-
W Voce	c Bradman b Fleetwood-Smith	0	1	1	-	-
Extras	(3 lb)	3				
Total	(all out, 78.6 overs)	323				

Fall of wickets:

1-29 (Barnett), 2-65 (Worthington), 3-117 (Hammond), 4-155 (Ames), 5-179 (Hardstaff), 6-195 (Allen), 7-306 (Robins), 8-322 (Verity), 9-323 (Sims), 10-323 (Voce)

Australia bowling	Overs	Mdns	Runs	Wkts	Wides	No-Balls
Sievers	12	2	39	1	-	-
McCabe	8	0	32	0	-	-

O'Reilly	21	6	65	3	-	-
Fleetwood-Smith	25.6	2	124	5	-	-
Ward	12	1	60	1	-	-

Scorecard Courtesy www.cricketarchive.com

129

Yorkshire v Nottinghamshire County Championship 1932

Venue	Headingley, Leeds on 9th, 11th, 12th July 1932 (3-day match)
Balls per over	6
Toss	Nottinghamshire won the toss and decided to bat
Result	Yorkshire won by 10 wickets
Points	Yorkshire 15; Nottinghamshire 0
Umpires	HG Baldwin, W Reeves
Scorer	W Ringrose (Yorkshire)

Close of play day 1 Nottinghamshire (1) 234 all out

Close of play day 2 Yorkshire (1) 163/9 (Macaulay 8*, Bowes 1*)

Nottinghamshire first innings		Runs	Balls	Mins	4s
WW Keeton	b Rhodes	9			
FW Shipston	b Macaulay	8			
W Walker	c Barber b Bowes	36			
*AW Carr	c Barber b Verity	0			
A Staples	b Macaulay	3			
CB Harris	lbw b Leyland	35			
GV Gunn	b Verity	31			
+B Lilley	not out	46			
H Larwood	b Leyland	48			
W Voce	b Leyland	0			
SJ Staples	b Leyland	0			
Extras	(8 b, 6 lb, 2 nb, 2 w)	18			
Total	(all out, 132.2 overs)	234			

Fall of wickets:

1-15, 2-35, 3-40, 4-46, 5-67, 6-120, 7-159, 8-233, 9-233, 10-234 (132.2 ov)

Yorkshire bowling	Overs	Mdns	Runs	Wkts	Wides	No-Balls
Bowes	31	9	55	1	-	-
Rhodes	28	8	49	1	-	-
Verity	41	13	64	2	-	-
Macaulay	24	10	34	2	-	-
Leyland	8.2	3	14	4	-	-

Yorkshire first innings		Runs	Balls	Mins	4s	6s
P Holmes	b Larwood	65				

H Sutcliffe	c Voce b Larwood	0
A Mitchell	run out	24
M Leyland	b Voce	5
W Barber	c and b Larwood	34
*AB Sellers	b A Staples	0
+A Wood	b Larwood	1
AC Rhodes	c A Staples b Voce	3
H Verity	b Larwood	12
GG Macaulay	not out	8
WE Bowes	not out	1
Extras	(5 b, 5 lb)	10
Total	(9 wickets, declared, 62 overs)	163

Fall of wickets:

1-1, 2-37, 3-122, 4-123, 5-125, 6-128, 7-135, 8-152, 9-154

Nottinghamshire bowling	Overs	Mdns	Runs	Wkts	Wides	No-Balls
Larwood	22	4	73	5	-	-
Voce	22	2	52	2	-	-
SJ Staples	7	2	8	0	-	-
A Staples	11	3	20	1	-	-

Nottinghamshire second innings		Runs	Balls	Mins	4s
WW Keeton	c Macaulay b Verity	21			
FW Shipston	c Wood b Verity	21			
W Walker	c Macaulay b Verity	11			
*AW Carr	c Barber b Verity	0			
A Staples	c Macaulay b Verity	7			
CB Harris	c Holmes b Verity	0			
GV Gunn	lbw b Verity	0			
+B Lilley	not out	3			
H Larwood	c Sutcliffe b Verity	0			
W Voce	c Holmes b Verity	0			
SJ Staples	st Wood b Verity	0			
Extras	(3 b, 1 nb)	4			
Total	(all out, 47.4 overs)	67			

Fall of wickets:

1-44, 2-47, 3-51, 4-63, 5-63, 6-63, 7-64, 8-64, 9-67, 10-67 (47.4 ov)

131

Yorkshire bowling	Overs	Mdns	Runs	Wkts	Wides	No-Balls
Bowes	5	0	19	0	-	-
Macaulay	23	9	34	0	-	-
Verity	19.4	16	10	10	-	-

Yorkshire second innings		Runs	Balls	Mins	4s	6s
P Holmes	not out	77				
H Sutcliffe	not out	54				
A Mitchell	did not bat					
M Leyland	did not bat					
W Barber	did not bat					
*AB Sellers	did not bat					
+A Wood	did not bat					
AC Rhodes	did not bat					
H Verity	did not bat					
GG Macaulay	did not bat					
WE Bowes	did not bat					
Extras	(4 b, 4 lb)	8				
Total	(no wicket, 40.4 overs)	139				

Nottinghamshire bowling	Overs	Mdns	Runs	Wkts	Wides	No-Balls
Larwood	3	0	14	0	-	-
Voce	10	0	43	0	-	-
SJ Staples	18.4	5	37	0	-	-
A Staples	6	1	25	0	-	-
Harris	3	0	12	0	-	-

Scorecard Courtesy www.cricketarchive.com

Bengal v Assam Ranji Trophy 1956/57 (East Zone)

Venue	National Sports Council of Assam Ground, Jorhat on 26th, 27th, 28th, 29th January 1957 (4-day match)
Balls per over	6
Toss	Toss not known
Result	Bengal won by an innings and 206 runs
Close of play day 1	Bengal (1) ?/?
Close of play day 2	Assam (1) 15/4 (Guha Roy 4*, Girdhari 2*)
Close of play day 3	Assam (2) 167/3 (Guha Roy ?*, Girdhari 69*)

Bengal first innings		Runs	Balls	Mins	4s
*P Roy	b Girdhari	30			
SM Basu Thakur	c Gogoi b Girdhari	16			
R Sanyal	b Girdhari	6			
DG Phadkar	c D Barua b Girdhari	51			
+PK Sen	c and b Rajbanshi	83			
RM Chanda	c Talukdar b Girdhari	32			
K Mitter	c D Barua b Rajbanshi	30			
SK Shome	b Girdhari	122			
SN Ghoshal	b Girdhari	46			
KK Biswas	not out	69			
PM Chatterjee	lbw b Rajbanshi	5			
Extras		15			
Total	(all out, 163.4 overs)	505			

Fall of wickets:

1-42, 2-49, 3-61, 4-168, 5-202, 6-253, 7-257, 8-339, 9-484, 10-505 (163.4 ov)

Assam bowling	Overs	Mdns	Runs	Wkts	Wides	No-Balls
Rajbanshi	62.4	7	213	3	-	-
Das	11	0	38	0	-	-
Girdhari	72	15	157	7	-	-
Guha Roy	4	0	19	0	-	-
D Barua	5	0	29	0	-	-
Hazarika	2	0	8	0	-	-
MP Barua	7	0	26	0	-	-

Assam first innings		Runs	Balls	Mins	4s	6s
A Guha Roy	c Shome b Chatterjee	4				
KK Baishya	lbw b Chatterjee	1				
MP Barua	b Chatterjee	2				
*D Barua	lbw b Chatterjee	2				
A Hazarika	b Chatterjee	0				
SK Girdhari	lbw b Chatterjee	14				
S Gogoi	b Chatterjee	4				
TK Barua	b Chatterjee	5				
A Rajbanshi	b Chatterjee	0				
+M Talukdar	not out	2				
G Das	b Chatterjee	0				
Extras		20				
Total	(all out, 38 overs)	54				

Fall of wickets:

1-4, 2-8, 3-12, 4-12, 5-15, 6-29, 7-45, 8-45, 9-54, 10-54 (38 ov)

Bengal bowling	Overs	Mdns	Runs	Wkts	Wides	No-Balls
Chatterjee	19	11	20	10	-	-
Phadkar	14	12	10	0	-	-
Biswas	4	2	4	0	-	-
Shome	1	1	0	0	-	-

Assam second innings (following on)		Runs	Balls	Mins	4s	6s
TK Barua	b Ghoshal	21				
+M Talukdar	lbw b Phadkar	0				
KK Baishya	c Chatterjee b Phadkar	42				
A Guha Roy	c Ghoshal b Phadkar	12				
SK Girdhari	c Biswas b Phadkar	100				
A Hazarika	c and b Ghoshal	10				
*D Barua	c Roy b Phadkar	0				
S Gogoi	c Mitter b Phadkar	3				
MP Barua	c and b Phadkar	1				
A Rajbanshi	c Chatterjee b Ghoshal	9				
G Das	not out	4				
Extras		43				
Total	(all out, 107.5 overs)	245				

Fall of wickets:

1-4, 2-77, 3-79, 4-175, 5-195, 6-209, 7-215, 8-219, 9-229, 10-245 (107.5 ov)

Bengal bowling	Overs	Mdns	Runs	Wkts	Wides	No-Balls
Phadkar	35	6	65	7	-	-
Chatterjee	28	14	38	0	-	-
Biswas	11	3	25	0	-	-
Shome	6	1	15	0	-	-
Ghoshal	22.5	9	42	3	-	-
Sanyal	4	0	15	0	-	-
Basu Thakur	1	0	2	0	-	-

Scorecard Courtesy www.cricketarchive.com

Ireland v West Indians - West Indies in British Isles 1969

Venue   Holm Field, Sion Mills on 2nd July 1969 (1-day single innings match)

Balls per over 6

Toss   West Indians won the toss and decided to bat

Result   Ireland won by 9 wickets

Umpires   M Stott, A Tichett

West Indians innings		Runs	Balls	Mins	4s	6s
GS Camacho	c Dineen b Goodwin	1				
MC Carew	c Hughes b O'Riordan	0				
MLC Foster	run out	2				
*BF Butcher	c Duffy b O'Riordan	2				
CH Lloyd	c Waters b Goodwin	1				
CL Walcott	c Anderson b O'Riordan	6				
JN Shepherd	c Duffy b Goodwin	0				
+TM Findlay	c Waters b Goodwin	0				
GC Shillingford	not out	9				
PR Roberts	c Colhoun b O'Riordan	0				
PD Blair	b Goodwin	3				
Extras	(1 b)	1				
Total	(all out, 25.3 overs)	25				

Fall of wickets:

1-1, 2-1, 3-3, 4-6, 5-6, 6-8, 7-12, 8-12, 9-12, 10-25 (25.3 ov)

Ireland bowling	Overs	Mdns	Runs	Wkts	Wides	No-Balls
O'Riordan	13	8	18	4	-	-
Goodwin	12.3	8	6	5	-	-

Ireland innings		Runs	Balls	Mins	4s	6s
RHC Waters	c Findlay b Blair	2				
DR Pigot	c Camacho b Shillingford	37				
MS Reith	lbw b Shepherd	10				
J Harrison	lbw b Shepherd	0				
IJ Anderson	c Shepherd b Roberts	7				

PJ Dineen	b Shepherd	0
AJ O'Riordan	c and b Carew	35
GAA Duffy	not out	15
LP Hughes	c sub (VA Holder) b Carew	13
*DE Goodwin	did not bat	
+OD Colhoun	did not bat	
Extras	(2 lb, 4 nb)	6
Total	(8 wickets, declared, 47.2 overs)	125

Fall of wickets:

1-19, 2-30, 3-34, 4-51, 5-55, 6-69, 7-103, 8-125 (47.2 ov)

West Indians bowling	**Overs**	**Mdns**	**Runs**	**Wkts**	**Wides**	**No-Balls**
Blair	8	4	14	1	-	-
Shillingford	7	2	19	1	-	-
Shepherd	13	4	20	3	-	-
Roberts	16	3	43	1	-	-
Carew	3.2	0	23	2	-	-

West Indians innings		**Runs**	**Balls**	**Mins**	**4s**	**6s**
GS Camacho	c Dineen b Goodwin	1				
MC Carew	c Pigot b Duffy	25				
MLC Foster	c Pigot b Goodwin	0				
*BF Butcher	c Waters b Duffy	50				
CH Lloyd	not out	0				
CL Walcott	not out	0				
JN Shepherd	did not bat					
+TM Findlay	did not bat					
GC Shillingford	did not bat					
PR Roberts	did not bat					
PD Blair	did not bat					
Extras	(2 lb)	2				
Total	(4 wickets, 34 overs)	78				

Fall of wickets:

1-1, 2-1, 3-73, 4-78

Ireland bowling	**Overs**	**Mdns**	**Runs**	**Wkts**	**Wides**	**No-Balls**
O'Riordan	6	1	21	0	-	-

137

Goodwin	2	1	1	2	-	-
Hughes	7	4	10	0	-	-
Duffy	12	8	12	2	-	-
Anderson	7	1	32	0	-	-

Scorecard Courtesy www.cricketarchive.com

India in Australia 1991/92 (3rd Test)

Venue	Sydney Cricket Ground, Sydney on 2nd, 3rd, 4th, 5th, 6th January 1992 (5-day match)
Balls per over	6
Toss	India won the toss and decided to field
Result	Match drawn
Umpires	PJ McConnell, SG Randell
Referee	PBH May
Close of play day 1	Australia (1) 234/4 (Boon 89*, Border 14*)
Close of play day 2	India (1) 103/2 (Shastri 52*, Vengsarkar 13*)
Close of play day 3	India (1) 178/2 (Shastri 95*, Vengsarkar 43*)
Close of play day 4	India (1) 445/7 (Tendulkar 120*, Pandit 3*)
Man of the Match	RJ Shastri

Australia first innings		Runs	Balls	Mins	4s	6s
GR Marsh	b Banerjee	8	48	54	1	-
MA Taylor	c Pandit b Banerjee	56	135	207	5	-
DC Boon	not out	129	361	444	13	-
ME Waugh	c Prabhakar b Banerjee	5	10	14	1	-
DM Jones	run out	35	75	99	4	-
*AR Border	c Pandit b Kapil Dev	19	51	67	2	-
+IA Healy	c sub (K Srikkanth) b Prabhakar	1	4	6	-	-
MG Hughes	c Pandit b Prabhakar	2	5	10	-	-
CJ McDermott	b Prabhakar	1	7	14	-	-
SK Warne	c Pandit b Kapil Dev	20	67	71	1	-
BA Reid	c Tendulkar b Kapil Dev	0	2	1	-	-
Extras	(4 b, 14 lb, 18 nb, 1 w)	37				
Total	(all out, 499 minutes, 124 overs)	313				

Fall of wickets:

1-22 (Marsh), 2-117 (Taylor), 3-127 (Waugh), 4-210 (Jones), 5-248 (Border), 6-251 (Healy), 7-259 (Hughes), 8-269 (McDermott), 9-313 (Warne), 10-313 (Reid, 124 ov)

India bowling	Overs	Mdns	Runs	Wkts	Wides	No-Balls
Kapil Dev	33	9	60	3	-	-
Prabhakar	39	12	82	3	-	-

Banerjee	18	4	47	3	-	-
Srinath	21	5	69	0	-	-
Shastri	13	1	37	0	-	-

India first innings

India first innings		Runs	Balls	Mins	4s	6s
RJ Shastri	c Jones b Warne	206	477	572	17	2
NS Sidhu	c Waugh b McDermott	0	7	11	-	-
SV Manjrekar	c Waugh b Hughes	34	121	161	2	-
DB Vengsarkar	c Waugh b McDermott	54	140	196	3	-
*M Azharuddin	c Boon b McDermott	4	2	2	1	-
SR Tendulkar	not out	148	213	298	14	-
M Prabhakar	c Taylor b Hughes	14	29	42	1	-
Kapil Dev	c Marsh b Hughes	0	1	1	-	-
+CS Pandit	run out	9	18	32	-	-
ST Banerjee	c Border b McDermott	3	7	13	-	-
J Srinath	run out	1	2	7	-	-
Extras	(1 b, 4 lb, 5 nb)	10				
Total	(all out, 672 minutes, 168.4 overs)	483				

Fall of wickets:

1-7 (Sidhu), 2-86 (Manjrekar), 3-197 (Vengsarkar), 4-201 (Azharuddin), 5-397 (Shastri), 6-434 (Prabhakar), 7-434 (Kapil Dev), 8-458 (Pandit), 9-474 (Banerjee), 10-483 (Srinath, 168.4 ov)

Australia bowling	Overs	Mdns	Runs	Wkts	Wides	No-Balls
McDermott	51	12	147	4	-	-
Reid	4	0	10	0	-	-
Hughes	41.4	8	104	3	-	-
Waugh	14	5	28	0	-	-
Warne	45	7	150	1	-	-
Border	13	3	39	0	-	-

Australia second innings

Australia second innings		Runs	Balls	Mins	4s	6s
MA Taylor	c Kapil Dev b Shastri	35	122	182	-	-
GR Marsh	c Pandit b Kapil Dev	4	9	16	-	-
DC Boon	c Azharuddin b Srinath	7	33	36	-	-
ME Waugh	lbw b Prabhakar	18	51	50	-	-
DM Jones	c Pandit b Shastri	18	25	40	1	-
*AR Border	not out	53	157	158	2	-

+IA Healy	c Prabhakar b Shastri	7	28	36	-	-
MG Hughes	c Prabhakar b Tendulkar	21	73	76	1	-
CJ McDermott	c Vengsarkar b Shastri	0	5	10	-	-
SK Warne	not out	1	7	7	-	-
BA Reid	did not bat					
Extras	(4 lb, 4 nb, 1 w)	9				
Total	(8 wickets, 305 minutes, 84 overs)	173				

Fall of wickets:

1-9 (Marsh), 2-31 (Boon), 3-55 (Waugh), 4-85 (Jones), 5-106 (Taylor), 6-114 (Healy), 7-164 (Hughes), 8-171 (McDermott)

India bowling Overs Mdns Runs Wkts Wides No-Balls

	Overs	Mdns	Runs	Wkts	Wides	No-Balls
Kapil Dev	19	5	41	1	-	-
Prabhakar	27	10	53	1	-	-
Srinath	12	0	28	1	-	-
Shastri	25	8	45	4	-	-
Tendulkar	1	0	2	1	-	-

Notes

--> SK Warne made his debut in Test matches
--> ST Banerjee made his debut in Test matches
--> ST Banerjee made his last appearance in Test matches

Scorecard Courtesy www.cricketarchive.com

Please follow my writing and recommended reads on

www.cricketwriter.com

I can also be followed on Twitter **@Cric_Writer**

See you in the Autumn of 2017 with *Spell-binding Spells*.

Printed in Great Britain
by Amazon